Ranjit Lal is the author of forty-five books—fiction and non-fiction—for children and adults who are children. His abiding interest in natural history, birds, animals and insects is reflected in many of his books: *The Little Ninja Sparrows*, *Owlet, Not Out*, *The Crow Chronicles*, *The Life and Times of Altu Faltu*, *The Small Tigers of Shergarh*, *The Birds of Delhi*, *The Tigers of Taboo Valley* and others. His other books with social themes include *Faces in the Water*, *Our Nana Was a Nutcase*, *Taklu and Shroom*, *Miracles*, *Smitten*, *The Secret of Falcon Heights*, *The Dugong and the Barracudas* and *The Battle for No. 19*. He enjoys photography, reading and cooking. He lives in Delhi.

Also by Ranjit Lal

In Speaking Tiger (YA)
The Hidden Palace Adventure
What Lies Between Two Hearts

In Talking Cub
The Little Ninja Sparrows
Owlet, Not Out

Ranjit Lal

Illustrated by Kavita Singh Kale

SPEAKING TIGER BOOKS LLP
125A, Ground Floor, Shahpur Jat,
Near Asiad Village, New Delhi - 110 049

First published in paperback by Speaking Tiger Books in 2023

Copyright © Ranjit Lal 2023
Illustration copyright © Speaking Tiger Books 2023

ISBN: 978-93-5447-578-8
eISBN: 978-93-5447-580-1

10 9 8 7 6 5 4 3 2 1

The moral right of the author has been asserted.

No part of this publication may be reproduced, transmitted, or stored in a retrieval system, in any form or by any means, electronic, mechanical, photocopying, recording or otherwise, without the prior permission of the publisher.

This book is sold subject to the condition that it shall not, by way of trade or otherwise, be lent, resold, hired out, or otherwise circulated, without the publisher's prior consent, in any form of binding or cover other than that in which it is published.

Contents

Introduction	1
Ants: Getting Antsy	11
Termites: Crash and Burn	19
Cockroaches: Roaches Rule	25
Beetles: Beetlemania	33
Praying Mantis: 'I Love You So Much I'm Going to Eat You'	51
Dragonflies and Damselflies: Dragons from the Deep	57
Butterflies: Pretty Airheads or Steely Stunners?	63
Moths: Dancing After Dark	73
Bees: Oh, Honey, Honey	83
Wasps: The Bees' Diabolical Cousins	95
Bugs: Snug as a Bug in a Rug	109
Flies: Swat That Fly	119
Mosquitoes: Sirens of Death	129

Grasshoppers: The Grass is Zinging	139
Spiders: Spyder, Spyder, Hairy Fright	149
Scorpions: The Sting is in the Tail	161
Snails: There's a Slow Snail Coming	169
Centipedes and Millipedes: A Hundred, Thousand Feet	179
Head lice, Worms and Leeches: Horrible Houseguests	187
Ticks and Fleas: Appalling Animal Lovers	199
Afterword	209
Ranjit's Creepy Crawly Facts	213

Introduction

We see them here,
We see them there,
Creepy crawlies everywhere…

In our food and in our hair,
Creepy crawlies everywhere,
Some make us sick, some make us well
Some will make us run like hell.

Without them we would go extinct
On the double, pretty quick
Thank God we see them here and there
Creepy crawlies everywhere.

They've bitten us, stung us, devoured our food, infected us, disgusted us and given us the heebie-jeebies and sleepless nights as they wail in our ear. We swat them, spray them, and go to war on them with planes and drones. But attacks on them only make them immune all too soon, and they come back at us, better armed and more belligerent.

At the same time, they've dazzled us, mystified us, enthralled us, astounded us and shown us quite clearly that they're in charge of running and maintaining Planet Earth.

Who are they? They are creepy crawlies all: insects, spiders, snails, worms—crawlers, jumpers, fliers, wrigglers, singers, builders and runners. They're bizarre and beautiful, and we encounter them willy-nilly every single day. Like it or not, indoors or outdoors, they are our neighbours, house guests, squatters, and invaders, availing of our hospitality and often making us pay for it, whether we want to or not. Some, like mosquitoes, make deadly enemies indeed, killing us in our millions through diseases like malaria and dengue, while at the same time guarding precious tropical rainforests from our chainsaws. Mostly, however, creepy crawlies leave us alone. In turn, we rob them of the fruits of their toil and take advantage of their love lives to grow our crops and use them to turn waste into rich, fruity soil.

They have amazing lifestyles and life cycles and we still don't know how many million species there are. There are estimated to be 20 to 30 million species of insects alone, comprising 80 to 85 per cent of all living species. Some change from gluttons to skimpy sippers of nectar, some are equipped with 30,000 lenses in their eyes (all the better to see you with!) some emerge from underwater like dragons of the deep, some wear camouflage fatigues that commandos would envy. Some live and love in dung, while others eat their children and husbands, some wear the most glamorous outfits imaginable, some can jump over the equivalent of skyscrapers, some leave Hogan the Hulk looking like a wimp, and some may be both boys and girls at the same time!

We're going to meet them in this book: ants, cockroaches, butterflies, dragonflies, beetles, termites, shield bugs, earthworms, bees, wasps, dung-beetles, flies, crickets, grasshoppers, spiders, scorpions, fireflies, mosquitoes, slugs and snails et al.

After all, it's good to get to know the neighbours!

It's believed insects evolved somewhere between 300 and 350 million years ago and they have some remarkable qualities. They wear their hard skeletons (made of a substance called chitin), like a knight's armour outside their bodies. This makes them tough, waterproof and provides excellent protection when dropped from great heights (without the deafening clang that would occur if you dropped a knight from a similar height). They were the first to fly, using either two wings or four. An early dragonfly had a wingspan of over two and a half feet! Flight enabled them to get around, escape enemies and hunt down prey. Their relatively small size meant they hardly left any eco-footprint at all individually, though large swarms like locusts could devastate entire landscapes.

They spend more time as larvae and nymphs, with radically different lifestyles—and appetites—from their adult versions. They can choose whether to have boys or girls and usually it's the ladies that rule the roost. And as everyone knows, they have three main body parts—head, thorax and abdomen—and six legs.

Spiders belong to the sinister arachnid clan (along with such lovelies as ticks and scorpions). They have two body segments and eight legs, while centipedes and millipedes have several, the last perhaps 300 pairs of legs. (Wouldn't a shoe salesman faint with ecstasy when a millipede walks into his shop and says, 'I need new shoes, I've outgrown these!')

While I will still whack a mosquito wailing dengue in my ear and will launch an all-out attack on a centipede in the shower with a toilet brush, I've grown tolerant of most creepy crawlies. I'm still revolted by tiny squirming critters in old flour or horrible white worms wriggling out of guavas, but I benignly eye the tiny red ants that have died a gloriously sweet death en masse in a honey jar, and just spoon them out. I will back away from belligerent wasps and stay away from bees, but can watch a spider weave her trap for hours. I just love the fierce little jumping spiders with their bright, black eyes and boxer's moves. I can watch dragonflies patrol their airspace and swoop on interlopers like World War One fighters and think of how butterflies, which surely fly drunk, manage to touch down perfectly on a bloom. Caterpillars in jam jars that finally emerge from their chrysalis as newly minted butterflies–it's something you will never forget. As for the most successful villains of them all—cockroaches— they were among the earliest of insects to evolve. Today, these handsome dudes are likely to be the only survivors of a nuclear holocaust. That's why they're forever gleefully waving us goodbye with those feelers of theirs!

Why and how should you be interested in tiny creatures that either scuttle or fly away at your approach or make an infernal nuisance of themselves? Flies will buzz irritatingly around you and then settle just on the morsel you were about to put into your mouth, cockroaches will scuttle gleefully into dark nooks the moment you switch on the kitchen lights like boarding school kids caught smoking at a midnight party. At some point during your early morning walks you will have barged into a spider's web, and at home will fiercely sweep the cobwebs from the corners. So certainly, you can't miss them but how do you engage with them?

Well, all you actually need is a small dose of curiosity and inquisitiveness—the kind you show when you know the neighbours are having a marital showdown behind their muslin curtains! Be a voyeur and eavesdropper and keep asking yourself the question WHY.

My curiosity about butterflies really took flight when I spotted a bird-dropping move on the leaf of a kumquat plant. Closer inspection revealed it to be a small caterpillar. The penny dropped: birds love caterpillars—high protein for their young—but which bird would be caught dead picking up what looked like its own droppings?

Then, take flies: how the heck do they manage all those flight stunts, landing unerringly upside down on the ceiling? In the pool I took to playing lifeguard to the big black ants that floundered in the water; grandly picking them up and taking them out, even giving them the kiss of life by gently breathing over them! For most alas it was too late but then I noticed that out of nowhere a relay of little black ants turned up, scurrying at top speed seemingly helter-skelter, and shouting at one another. Then I noticed that one of the big dead ants had begun moving: a little one had got a hold of it rather like a tug does while pulling an Airbus or 747 out of its parking bay and was dragging it. Others quickly joined in and they lugged the big black ant into a crevasse at the corner of the pool, which was the entrance to their colony. They seemed to be working chaotically, everyone yelling and running around at random but there was a method to their madness and they hauled the huge ant into the tiny overhung entrance to their colony: one slip-up and the ant and many little ones would have landed in the pool. I showed this to my sister and she was fascinated so we fished out all sorts of dead little insects from the pool and the little ants feasted that day!

So, guaranteed you will not be bored! Birders usually get hugely excited when they see what they call a 'lifer': a bird they haven't seen before despite the fact that at one time in their lives a crow would have also have been a lifer. They run around excitedly telling one and all about their accomplishment. Well, watch insects and you can be pretty sure you'll be seeing a lifer every time you do so because there are so many kinds of them around. Thanks to the Internet there's a whole lot of information out there but remember we still know squat about so many species, or even of their existence.

If you do want to search them out, then mid-mornings and afternoons are usually the best time. Insects and arachnids are cold blooded and need the sun's warmth to get active. We're lucky in India because in most places it gets warm pretty early, so there's no need to stagger around in the midday heat. If you really get hooked you can put down a cotton sheet or even a plastic one under a bush and vigorously shake it and check out what falls on the sheet.

Beware, do make sure there are no wasp nests or beehives in the bush before you agitate it! You'll be surprised how many little creatures fall out of the bush. Never do anything as foolish as to toss a pebble into a beehive or a wasps' nest or probe a hole with a stick! Insects at home do not like being fingered. I've watched a common yellow wasp follow my movements from a distance of ten feet away: her implacable eyes never left me as I tried getting closer and closer as she guarded the entrance to her hole. As I moved from side to side, she swayed too, like a cobra, following me.

Early morning can be pretty rewarding too. If it is dewy there are sure to be webs strung like precious pearl necklaces hanging from every bush or tree. Walk slowly through the tall grass and you might come across a dragonfly, its beautiful wings bejewelled and you can admire it for as long as you like because it's frozen stiff and not going anywhere until the sun powers up its mighty flight muscles.

For moths and other night-outers, keep a porch light on all night and watch as they sashay up to dance the night away. Or switch on any bright light and again lay a sheet down beside it. Out of the dark a host of moths will shimmer out ready to party along with ponderous rhinoceros beetles, praying mantids and many more. I've never really done this myself because there's always been enough fare on the walls beneath say a porch light. Yes, there may be an issue if you live in a big, brightly blazing city because of light pollution, but if you ever go upcountry, or to a hill station or anywhere where the nights are velvety dark, you'll be well rewarded. As for spiders, well just hang around near a web and watch what comes by—and flies straight into it!

Photographing creepy crawlies can be tricky. For one they are so small. Secondly, they are forever on the move and move fast. You will need a macro lens, maybe a good flash, and magnum doses of patience. Autofocus and digital cameras have made things easier, but it still is challenging. Sometimes manual focussing can be better. With macro-photography you often get a very small portion of your subject in focus because of the narrow depth of field—a small aperture is necessary and flash will help you set one and also freeze motion. Try and focus on the eye that is closest to you.

If you hang around a flowering bush—the evil lantana is a favourite with butterflies—you are sure to catch your subjects. Not only butterflies, but bees, iridescent flies, and maybe waiting like a chinless assassin, the praying mantis. Dragonflies will every so often land on stalks to rest, then fly off and come back, sometimes chomping on prey they have caught on the wing. Mark these stalks out, focus on them and just wait. If they fly low and close enough (and even at you if you invade their airspace) you might even get them in flight. Long ago I tried photographing hoverflies in flight; this before the digital age. I spent a fortune on the amount of expensive film I consumed and 99 per cent of the shots went into the bin. But it was exhilarating and worth those couple of shots that came out okay.

For simple creepy-crawly watching you don't need any special equipment: just your eyes (a small pair of binoculars if you have them) and perhaps a lupe or magnifying glass if you want to take a closer look. There are enough fascinations in the world of creepy crawlies to last many lifetimes!

This happened when I was about seven or eight years old. There had been torrential rains, and a lake had burst its banks. The peepul tree that usually stood by the side of the lake was now stranded in the middle of the lake. I just had to make it to the big islanded tree standing in the middle of the flood. Gamely, I waded into the murky coffee-coloured water and made my way towards it. I was soon knee deep, my eyes scanning the water ahead for any crocodiles, pythons or piranhas making a beeline for me. Mercifully, there were none—but what was that: a flat, writhing raft, the size of a large paratha, fiery as red chillies, floating straight towards me? I drew close and peered at it—and then recoiled!

Tiny, viciously stinging red ants—maybe 10,000 of them—clinging together, flailing their legs and feelers and heading straight for me with single-minded intention. If they reached me, they would swarm up my shorts in a trice. I gave a squawk of alarm, turned around and fled back to the bank. I noticed now that more swarms of ants like these had been flooded out of their homes. No more heroic wading for me!

At some point we've all encountered ants—often painfully in parts of our bodies where they have no right to be. We've all opened jars of honey and jam to find a whole lot of them clustered thickly on the surface, having died a gloriously sweet death. If you ever climb a tree, you need to check you aren't violating the ants' highway code.

Ants have been around a long, long time—for around 168 million years. It's thought that there are at least 22,000 different types (species), of which around 12,500 have been identified, most living in the tropics (700 or so on the Indian subcontinent). For every one of us there are 1 million ants! However, it would take 40,000 ant brains to weigh as much as a single human brain.

Ants live in colonies which may have populations several million strong, and the entire colony functions as a single unit. Ant society is divided into three 'castes' each with its specific duties. At the top is the queen, whose sole purpose in life is to lay eggs like a factory's production line. She is fussed over by her daughters, 'workers' who feed her, tend to her, look after the eggs and pupae, clean the nest, throw out the garbage and guard against invaders. The few gentlemen that are around have only one purpose in life, though I don't think they mind it at all: When the queen thinks it's time to make a new colony she leaves the nest and flies out. Her daughters—the workers—are alas wingless, but the gentlemen, who are called drones, have wings. Off they go in pursuit in the hot humid night to mate with the queen. The happy couple returns to earth, the gentleman sheds his wings, wanders around and dies while the queen burrows into the ground and begins a new colony.

While most ants live in colonies, some like Africa's ferocious driver ants and South America's army ants are foragers. They set up teeming camps on the forest floor.

Battalions set forth, preceded by 'scouts' and hunting workers: everything alive they come across is fair game, from insects to birds to horses. Soldiers armed with formidable scissor-like mandibles stand guard as the columns march forth. They return to their bivouac with their spoils—food for hungry larvae and their queen. Once they clear an area of prey (they may take as many as 450,000 victims in a fortnight) the entire colony breaks camp carrying their queen and larvae along till they find another suitable hunting ground to set up camp again, or their queen wishes to lay her eggs. At a time the queen may lay 35,000 to 40,000 eggs.

Most ants live in colonies though, leaving the nest to forage for food. As we all know, they love sweets but will also take away grains, shoots, leaves, insects and any foodstuff we might leave out. If you've ever watched ants swarm over dead or dying insects, or small reptiles like geckos, you'll know how ruthless they are. I once witnessed a hunting party of shiny big black ants (the sort which swarm out during the rains) get after and take down a hefty carpenter bee. Like a pack of hunting dogs on the African savannah, they went after it, ripping its wings to shreds. The bee would rev full throttle, move a bit only to be set upon again, till it was literally taken apart.

The famous 'leaf cutter' ants saw off sections of leaves and take them to their nests—looking like a flotilla of tiny green sailboats—where they chew them up and fertilize with their droppings. A fungus forms on the leaves which the ants consume and feed to their larvae. Astonishingly, leaf cutters in the Amazon rainforest shift their nests to treetops when they sense that the forest floor is likely to get flooded. Some ants 'milk' aphids (which are plant pests) of sweet honeydew, a sugary waste product, and in turn protect them from predators.

When out foraging, ants leave a scent trail comprising of pheromones (chemical signals) which enables them to find their way back to the nest at the end of an expedition. These pheromones also lead other members of the colony to the find. To ensure that ants bring back the bacon so to speak, they have two stomachs: one for their own personal use and the second to provide food for the larvae and queen.

Pheromones have other uses too: if an ant is attacked or killed, it sends off special SOS pheromone signals which alerts the colony to the threat and enables them to prepare for action. Ants will and do go to war with each other; they raid each others' colonies, may kill the queen and take the larvae hostage, which, after they hatch are made to work as 'slaves' in the victor's colony.

Sometimes there may be two queens in a single colony, often resulting in power tussles: one queen will eventually kill her rival and reign supreme. In one species it was found that a queen deliberately allowed herself to be captured by the enemy, and once in the enemy camp set upon and killed the residing queen and took the reins of power! In another species, 'suicide' soldiers, when outnumbered by the enemy, set upon them and exploded like bombs, covering the enemy with toxic, sticky goo—bringing them to a sticky end. Both the brave soldier and the enemy die.

In another species it was found that after a battle, the ants would tend to their wounded and even take them back to their nests. But this, only if the injuries were not too serious and there was a chance of recovery. Badly wounded ants were left to die on the battlefield.

Sometimes blindly following orders—and scent trails in particular—can get you into trouble. Army ant columns sometimes 'double back' in their marches: the leaders blindly following their own pheromone trails, round and round and round. This is called an ant mill and they will do this till they die of exhaustion. I came across a similar phenomenon in my washroom! At 7 a.m. one morning, I found a big black ant walking along the rim of my soap dish. At 9 a.m. the lady was still at it, going round and round. At midday she was still going strong, though by 2 p.m. she had started staggering. I took pity on her and moved her off the plate: off she trundled happily, the swagger back in her step. On the rim of the plate, she had been blindly following her own trail, thinking it would lead her home!

Like us, ants also have immigration and passport control. Every member of a colony has its own particular pheromone which is recognized by other members: Especially by immigration control at the entrance of a nest, comprising formidable soldier ants who scrutinize the papers of every ant returning to the colony after a foraging expedition. I actually witnessed this, again with big black ants. The guards would touch feelers with the arrival, checking it out and only letting it in if its pheromones were in order! If not, the intruder would be attacked and sent packing.

Ant colonies are usually found underground though they may also nest in trees and even buildings. They help aerate the soil, recycle nutrients, get rid of pests, may be used as food (by us) and their toxins used to make medicines. The formidable scissor jaws of army ants have even been used as sutures by surgeons to close up wounds. The ant is placed at the edges of the wound held close together, they bite and clamp in place, closing the wound. And then alas, the surgeons cut off their bodies, leaving the clamped jaws in place, stapling shut the wound! (We really are a diabolical race!)

Ants can be pests too, spoiling food stocks and crops, even buildings. Most ants are armed with jaws and stings, sometimes poison-tipped with acid. Birds, in fact, take advantage of this acid: they will settle down on top of an ant nest and wriggle ecstatically, opening and closing their wings. The acid that the agitated ants squirt on them apparently kills the parasites that plague the birds. Ants themselves have enemies too: termites hate them, we exterminate them, and anteaters (and chimpanzees) scoop them up and slurp them down, as do birds.

These tireless workers are immensely strong: some can lift fifty to hundred times their own body weight—that's like me lifting a two and a half ton SUV!

They always seem to be in a tremendous hurry, speeding along ant 'highways', yet they never have a pile-up. If we could move equivalently fast we'd be like racehorses!

Ants usually live for forty-five to sixty days, though some queens have been known to go strong for as long as thirty years! But once the queen dies, the colony is doomed. For ants it's certainly a case of 'all for one, and one for all!'

Crash and Burn
(Termites)

Way back when I was a student in Bombay (now Mumbai), I often used to cram for the exams deep into the night in our huge verandah which overlooked the whole of Central Bombay. On fragrant monsoon nights it was pleasant and breezy and there were many happy distractions: thunder threatening in the distance, furry moths blundering in and being stalked by the geckos, flurries of rain and the great cane chicks flapping like the sails of galleons of yore. On particularly humid nights there could be visitors too: first one, then another and soon hundreds of wriggly brown insects flying in on slim transparent ochre wings and crashing headlong into the white hot table lamp to sizzle and fizz. Many landed on my textbooks, quickly shed their wings and wriggled frantically one after another. They were perhaps a little over half an inch in length, and looked a bit like tiny worms. In minutes I would be staring at a mass of them and hundreds of discarded wings blowing this way and that.

Termites! They came from some unknown termite castle on the cliff our apartment was perched on, romantic gentlemen and lady termites who had left their home in mass flights, only to be misguided by my table lamp, like a pirate's lantern luring ships onto the rocks…Normally, the insects would have paired off, landed on the good earth, and found themselves a suitable spot to burrow into the ground and establish a home. Here, the pair would be king and queen and having sealed their entrance, got on with their honeymoon and the business of raising a family. The queen would take it slow at first, laying perhaps ten or twenty eggs, one at a time, and both parents would take care of the young that hatched. Then, as this generation grew (from 'nymphs' to 'workers'), she would up the pace to maybe 2000 to 3000 eggs per day—relying on her older children to care for the younger ones—just as is done in any large family. Soon, the colony would be established—teeming with maybe a million busybodies. The lifespan of a colony could be fifteen to twenty years, that of workers, two to five years.

Termites are thought to be the first insects to establish a caste system in their societies, some 100 million years ago. At the top are the king and queen, who can live for as many as sixty to seventy years and who are forever faithful to one another. Then there are, what was called the 'supplementary reproductives'—ladies and gentlemen who could have children in case something terrible happened to the reigning monarchs. It is also this lot that occasionally leave the nest on cool monsoon nights to seek a kingdom for themselves. Soldiers—armed with massive jaws—take care of security concerns and workers do all the chores of raising the young, tending to their fungus gardens, repairs and maintenance of the castle. Neither of these two 'castes' can breed and both are usually blind. Like ants, they communicate by touch (antennae) and through pheromones, using different ones for different purposes.

Termites are also called 'white ants', though they're not related to ants, but more so to cockroaches and mantids. So far, over 3000 species have been identified of which 700 or so can be found in India. Here, they're called 'deemak' and the word often strikes terror in the hearts of homeowners in India as does its English equivalent elsewhere in the world. For termites have the singular ability to eat and digest wood— houses made of wood, furniture, trees, any wooden object that has been neglected for a while. They process the cellulose in the wood (the most indigestible part) and convert it into sugars, which they feed to the white fungus they cultivate in 'farms' which in turn is fertilized by their dung—and feed to their larvae. And they're clever. While they go about their furniture or house wrecking, they'll attack the insides first, leaving the outer veneer intact so you don't know what's going on until you open a cupboard door only to find it crumble to powder in your hands! Unlike ants, they're vegans, eating dead plant matter, wood, leaf litter, fungus, humus and dung.

Termites are soft-bodied insects, missing the armoured 'exoskeleton' of ants and are very sensitive to sunlight—no sun-tanning for them. They live in labyrinths of tunnels deep underground and great 'mounds' made of cement-hard dung and mud. These massive medieval-looking mud forts may soar up to 8 or 9 metres high and are rock hard: try kicking one and you'll be hopping in pain. Their remarkable network of ducts, tunnels and 'chimneys' enables cool air to enter from the bottom and warm air to escape from the top, centrally 'air-conditioning' the forts.

Or else termites nest in trees, but whenever they have to emerge into the outdoors, will construct mud tunnels around themselves as they progress, so that they're not exposed to sunlight. (These are the 'runnels' you can often see on wooden fences and trunks of trees.) The soldiers, armed with massive mandibles, guard their fortresses, either by biting or even shooting (like some ants do) toxic guck over the enemy or simply jamming their massive heads against the entrance of their tunnels so that nothing can get past them. Ants are one implacable enemy and often ferocious ant armies will raid termite mounds, killing, consuming and taking away booty. Termite colonies too may go to war with each other and bodies of the dead are left in special cemetery chambers.

Strong as they are, these fortresses are no match for the great raking claws of a sloth bear or an anteater which will demolish them. But even as the fortress crumbles, workers will frantically get busy repairing the damage as quickly as they can. But then alas, neither are these insects a match for clever chimpanzees, who simply stick a long 'rod' (a suitable twig) down the tunnels and slurp up the furious soldiers bristling all over it. Also, when the massed 'honeymoon' flights take off, birds, bats, lizards and other insects wait in eager anticipation. Humans eat termites too, roasted and fried, and like most insects they're very high in protein.

Termites do damage crops, and our built structures, but also turn up the soil and make it recycle nutrients. In India, around forty species are considered harmful, in the world the tally stands at around 180 plus.

Granted, these mushy brown insects are not the most prepossessing as they wriggle around blindly, and we will yell for the exterminator the moment we see signs of them in our houses. But we must also remember that they're remarkable civil engineers too and have mastered the art of centrally air-conditioning their massive structures in a completely self-sustaining way.

Roaches Rule

(Cockroaches)

Imagine the scene: A dim, gloomy Intensive Cardiac Care Ward in a major government hospital. You are recovering from surgery: the entire left side of your chest has been cut open and stitched up in three places and there's a tube sticking out of your abdomen, draining fluids. You have watched an eleven-year-old street girl die gasping for breath in a bed in front of yours despite the frantic efforts of the doctors. The old man in the bed next to you appears to be next. You are not in the best of moods.

Ah, but now it is time for lunch! A ward boy enters carrying a stainless steel thali piled with food. He approaches your bed and thrusts the thali at you. There's a heap of rice, dal, some vegetables, a roti and…an absolutely gigantic brown cockroach walking along the rim of the thali, waving its feelers about, pausing to sample the fare. You point this out. The boy nods and casually flicks the roach off the thali on to the ground. It scuttles under your bed, into the sloshy bedpan kept there: possibly for a sip or two…

No wonder roaches revolt us! Horrendously, there are around 4600 species of them in the world, but mercifully only around thirty like to be around us. Most only roam our kitchens and bathrooms at night and will scuttle for cover when we switch on the lights. They'll help themselves to anything edible: bread, leather, book bindings, skin flakes, and even cellulose, leaving their distinct disgusting (and unhealthy) stench and dung behind. The pathogens in their poop (which give off the odour) can trigger allergic reactions in us, and set off asthmatic attacks in children. And yes, they love beer too, attracted by the sugars and hops. They bite and chew their food (thirty-two times, I wonder?) and have no offensive weapons like claws and barbs. But when things get really tough they will become cannibals: in order to eat, and to control their population. They are social insects, communicating with pheromones.

Cockroaches are the 'scavengers' of the insect kingdom—and who likes those? Sleep warily because they love the odour of earwax and will burrow deep into ears to snack: not a pleasant prospect for us. Also, they have been suspected of nibbling off the eyelashes of sleeping children and burrowing under toenails. Be warned: not all are afraid of the bright lights! Some giant winged cockroaches will fly straight out of the dark night into a brightly lit room and plant a smooch on the rosy cheek of the fair maiden you were just about to kiss yourself, like some jealous suitor. For you alas, it's downhill after that!

These old timers have been around for some 320 million years and are built like tanks. Their hard exoskeleton is wax coated and they can live headless for a week: the heads themselves surviving for several hours. They can go without food for a month, without air for forty-five minutes, though only three days without water. Some even live underwater, carrying their air supply in bubbles. While they love the warmth and humidity of the tropics and subtropics, they withstand freezing temperatures without a fuss. Most are reddish-brown or black, and around the size of a thumbnail, but there are whoppers that can be

2 inches long. They can withstand nuclear radiation up to fifteen times what we can and hence are believed to be one of the only living creatures that would survive nuclear Armageddon (fruit-flies are another). Needless to add, they develop immunity to pesticides very efficiently. Try and swat them with a magazine or rolled-up newspaper and you'll know just how fast they are: in human terms they can sprint at 200 mph! And they can squeeze into the narrowest gaps by compressing their bodies by half. Their soft, flexible membranes work like hinges. A 12 mm 'tall' cockroach can vanish into a 3 mm gap. They can withstand pressures of 300 to as much as 900 times their body weight. Scientists are now figuring ways they can achieve the same with cockroach 'bots': a contraption so small that can scuttle everywhere would be of great help in search and recover operations.

Cockroaches multiply fast and furiously: a couple can raise between 2 and 3 million babies in two years if given ideal child-care facilities. Some cockroaches lay eggs in cases and others give birth to live young. Incidentally, cockroaches are the only terrestrial creatures to have had babies in space—there goes our final frontier!

The four commonly encountered stalwarts are the American cockroach (the giant amongst them), the German (small, scuttles around in groups), Australian and Oriental (considered the dirtiest).

The best way to keep cockroaches away is to keep a spotless kitchen and bathroom. But would a world entirely without cockroaches be a healthier place? Not really, because that would properly mess up the vital nitrogen cycle in nature. By feeding on decaying organic material (dead and dying things) cockroaches via their poop 'free up' nitrogen which gets trapped in these creatures. This freed nitrogen in the poop, which becomes a part of the soil, is vital for the well-being of plant life: a forest, and everything in it, would die without it.

We really have slandered these insects and smeared their reputation. But if you take a dispassionate look at one of these creatures you will have to admit that it is quite handsome: its exoskeleton looks like polished mahogany, though admittedly its twirling feelers and small eyes will give you the heebie-jeebies: But there are many forest-dwelling species of cockroaches that are really quite beautiful.

Not everyone hates cockroaches. The curator of a natural history museum in America has been quoted saying, 'Butterflies are just cockroaches with wings'. Apparently there's a zoo in Japan where 'cockroach petting sessions' are held twice a week, and cockroach 'races' have been organized in countries around the world. As a schoolboy, I once kept cockroaches in my pockets and would offer them to girls as if they were chocolates, in order to gross them out—not a good way to win a popularity contest (or girlfriends) for sure.

Many people—men, women and children—develop major phobias against cockroaches; they freak out or just freeze when they spot one. Cockroaches are in fact the most feared insects in the world—and are harmless! But several societies around the world eat cockroaches too: in Thailand for example, you can have them lightly sautéed, deep fried, grilled, boiled and broiled. They're supposed to be crunchy on the outside and succulent on the inside! Like all insects, they're very high in protein and very nutritious. You can even enjoy a cup of cockroach tea! The Chinese believe that they have medicinal qualities. Cockroaches do have their predators too: lizards will gobble them up and there are wasps which sting and anesthetize them in order to lay an egg on them so that the larvae has fresh cockroach meat to eat when it emerges.

Like them or loathe them, one thing seems certain: We may come and we may go, but cockroaches go on forever!

Did God really have 'an inordinate fondness for beetles' as one famous biologist, a gentleman called Mr Haldane, claimed, tongue firmly in cheek because there are so many kinds of beetles—400,000 and counting—in the world? That's actually more than any other living species. They make up 40 per cent of all insects. Well God didn't really because he or she didn't make beetles in the first place: their very, very, very early ancestors began the process themselves—a process called evolution. Over a period of millions and millions of years, (earliest beetle fossils date back 250 million years) beetles were designed to live in every nook and cranny of planet Earth except in Antarctica and in the oceans, and eat every food available without a fuss. To ensure they survived in some of the cruelest, harshest places on Earth, they were built like tanks, protected by their tough 'elytra': forewings which fused and hardened and covered most of their bodies, and made them virtually indestructible. The elytra are also thought to function as ailerons, helping beetles to fly. But otherwise, beetles vary widely in shape, size, colour, design, defence armaments and eating habits.

There is a reason beetles can survive in almost every place on Earth. To get through tough winters 90 per cent of the species go into a sort of lockdown mode as the days begin to shorten, reducing their requirements to a bare minimum. They can survive between temperatures of -58 to 50 degrees Celsius by making their own anti-freeze, and conjuring water out of fog and mist!

Humans and beetles have a long relationship. While we've eaten as many as 344 species of beetles, mainly in snotty larval form, they can be massive crop pests too as also friends of the farmer. They've been used to make traditional 'medicines' none of which have been scientifically proven to be of any use. One infamous beetle (the Colorado potato beetle) was actually used as a weapon of war: let loose on the enemy's potato crops, presumably to starve the army!

I have described next some of the coolest beetles trundling around: from tiny tots that shine like jewels, to guys who fire their versions of the AK-47.

Dung-beetles: Roll, baby roll!

While walking in Delhi's Northern Ridge one evening, a movement on the path suddenly caught my eye. I bent down for a closer look and was completely delighted. A rotund, greeny-bronze beetle, with spade-like hindlegs was valiantly pushing a ball of dog doo-doo—a ball larger than him. He did a kind of handstand and shoved the ball backwards across the path with his hind legs. Naturally all traffic on the path had to be diverted until he got across safely! From time to time he'd stop, climb on top of the ball, swivel around to take his bearings and then resume pushing. Ever since I met this valiant little chap, the dung-beetle has been my all-time favourite beetle.

You'll be happy to know there's no shortage of them in the world (as there is no shortage of dung): there are as many as between 5000 and 8000 different species and they live everywhere. And yes, they all share a liking for dung (the fresher the better). Not very appetizing, you might think, but which makes them invaluable to us as they turn the smelly stuff emitted by livestock into fresh, nutritious soil. They've turned specialist too: dividing themselves up into 'rollers', 'tunnelers' and 'dwellers'.

My little friend was a roller. He'd roll his ball of dung to a soft spot and bury it, then his wife would lay her eggs in it so that her babies could get good wholesome food to eat (as would they). Sometimes dung-beetle couples work together: while the husband rolls the ball, the wife shouts directions and encouragement and helps if he has to push it up a slope. They have to be snappy, because other dung-beetles (which may hang around in gangs) are only too ready to snatch and grab. They've got an excellent sense of smell and thousands can home in on a fresh patty within minutes of it plopping to the ground. One account has it that as many as 4000 dung-beetles turned up to party on a patty of elephant dung, within fifteen minutes of it being delivered.

Anything from monkey poo to 50 lb. elephant bombs is manna from heaven for these beetles, though they seem to prefer the dung of vegans. While the adults slurp up the liquidy inside portions of the patty, the babies prefer the crusty exterior, so everyone's happy. In fact, Australians too ought to be very happy with, and eternally grateful to, dung-beetles. When the European settlers took their herds of livestock to Australia, the beasts completely zapped the native dung-beetles there. I've come across two versions of what happened, though both had the same end result.

The first was that the amount of dung deposited by the enormous herds of livestock completely overwhelmed the local Australian dung-beetles. Oh yes in the beginning, they tried their best, adapting from dry kangaroo pellets, but eventually as the herds grew gigantic, the beetles just couldn't deal with the quantities involved. So they presumably ate their fill and left the rest to rot and fester in the hot Australian sun, which in turn gave rise to clouds of unpleasant disease-spreading bush-flies, not good if you liked the outdoors life. The second version has it that the native Australian dung-beetles did not at all like the gooey melt-in-your-mouth cattle dung having been brought up on hard, dry kangaroo pellets, so refused to touch it. End result was the same: dung lying everywhere, threatening to get knee deep and breeding flies. So, Australian scientists set in motion Project Dung-beetle, which functioned between 1965 and 1988: They imported several species of dung-beetle from South Africa and Europe (and Asia according to one account) and tested them out. As many as twenty-three of the immigrant species dealt with the issue efficiently and so 1.73 million of them were let loose and now have solved Australia's dung problem. As a result, bush-fly populations have fallen by 90 per cent!

When a gentleman dung-beetle finds a treasure trove of dung, he begins to roll it into a ball, hoping to impress the girl of his dreams. Some can shove dung-balls up to fifty times their body weight and can bury 250 times their body weight in dung in a single night. If the lady thinks this is He-man enough she'll follow him (yelling encouragement one presumes) or help him. Some dung-beetles roll balls of dung as large as an apple or a tennis ball! Sometimes, while underground, gentlemen will joust and head-butt each other over the possession of a prized dung-ball and the lady-in-waiting.

Once the dung-ball is buried, the lady lays between three and twenty eggs in it and it is sealed with the parents' own dung and some mud. In some species, both mama and papa look after and protect the baby dung-beetles that finally hatch, really sweet because very few insects go in for tender parenting. Some small (and presumably insecure) dung-beetles actually live inside the bottoms of animals like apes, in anticipation of the formation of a doo-doo—agreed a disgusting place to hang out in, but what to do?

The ancient Egyptians were so impressed by these beetles that they worshipped them, believing that they represented God rolling the sun across the sky during the course of a day. Rollers are also known as sacred scarab beetles, dung chafers, or more delightfully, tumblebugs! In fact, they're also known to use the position of the sun and the Earth's magnetic field to find their way around. One species that works at night is suspected of using the Milky Way for this purpose, and another, the moon!

Tunnelers burrow deep into dung—wherever they find it—and don't try to take it anywhere. Here they are safe from parasitic freeloaders. Snug in the depths of their smelly home, the lady of the house checks out the parts that are her favourite while the gentleman shops around for favourite flavours in the dung. They are doting parents and will stay with their young for as many as four months. The holes the tunnelers dig prevent the formation of methane gas in the dung, which would otherwise bubble out and is bad for the environment.

Dwellers simply live on top of the dung pile, the lady lays her eggs here and the baby develops from larva to adult in these salubrious surroundings. They love cow patties the best.

And finally, one species, the horned dung-beetle, holds the record for the strongest beetle in the world. It can hoist 1141 times its own body weight, the equivalent of a man weighing 75 kg lifting around fourteen six-ton bull elephants!

Rhinoceros Beetle: Stegosaurus of the insect world

When I saw it trundling ponderously across the floor towards the screen door one monsoon night, I thought it had just waddled out of the set of *Jurassic Park*. It wore armour in maroon brown and sported a massive shiny black horn on its head, with another horn sticking out of its body. It looked indestructible. I knew it was a rhinoceros beetle, now title holder of the second strongest beetle in the world, capable of lifting 850 times its own weight, though some detractors have said that this claim is unsubstantiated. It is related to the famous scarab beetle clan of which the dung-beetles are a part too.

I glanced at the screen door and the reason for its evening walk became apparent. Clinging on to the wire mesh was a lady, who the gentleman obviously hoped to make his partner. She does not carry the impressive headgear of the gentleman. To help him out I tried prising the lady off the door so she could meet with the gent downstairs. She clung tenaciously to the door. I backed off. I knew she couldn't bite or sting, but I didn't want to injure her by pulling her off. She would meet her intended if cupid so desired...

Often however, two gents converge on the same lady, say up in the branches of a tree or bush. This is when they put their massive metallic-looking horns to good use, trying to lever them under each other and toss the rival off the tree to drop ignominiously to the ground below. They can injure one another quite severely in these battles and sometimes the poor lady suffers collateral damage too! If all goes well, she'll eventually lay about fifty eggs in a tree trunk and the larvae that hatch from these will subsist on a diet of rotting wood for a year or two, growing to the size of a massively chunky finger and weigh 100 grams. The beetle is pretty nutritious himself, consisting of 40 per cent protein (as against 20 per cent in chicken and 18 per cent in beef) and so a favourite with birds.

The largest of these beetles can grow to 6 inches or 15 cm in length. The rhinoceros beetles live on nectar, sap and fruit (fresh and rotting) and have a lifespan of two to three years. Rather than swaggering around terrorizing the neighourhood, they use their massive strength to dig themselves deep into the leaf litter or ground, to escape predators. They can fly, but with all that bulk to handle are not the most skilful aeronauts.

They are popular pets in some South Asian countries, and typically, men will bring two rival beetles together in the presence of a lady, to incite them to fight. And of course, bets are laid...

There are some 300 species worldwide and some of the rhinoceros beetle's gigantic cousins include the Hercules beetle, the Atlas beetle and the elephant beetle—their names being self explanatory.

Jewel Beetle: Jewel in the crown

While out for a walk in Kasauli many years ago, I felt something land on my hand and quickly took a look in case it was something nasty. It was a tiny rotund beetle, just folding its wings inside its elytra—and it blew me away! It shimmered a metallic emerald and red and purple as I looked at it from various angles. It looked like a tiny animated precious stone: it was a jewel beetle. Photographing it turned out to be trickier than I anticipated: its colours changed as you changed your viewpoint and you couldn't use flash which would bleach out all of its iridescence.

The beetle's shimmering iridescence serves as camouflage in the forests. It's orange, no, purple, no green...heck where did it go? Now you see it, now you don't!

I was happy to discover that there are quite a few jewel beetles around: some 15,500 species. They're also known less romantically as metallic wood boring beetles, which makes them sound like some kind of workman's tool. It's the wing cases, the elytra of these beetles that have the brilliant colours, and needless to say, these beetles are a great favourite with collectors who will pin them up like they do butterflies. In fact, in India and other Asian countries, intricate jewelry is also made out of their beautiful elytra.

Their larvae can bury themselves in roots, logs and even green wood, and some are serious pests. Some jewel beetles can smell out a forest fire burning 80 km away and will fly there to lay their eggs on smouldering wood, where they are safe from predators. Jewel beetles may be between 3 and 80 mm long and its always worthwhile keeping a lookout for these shining jewels in the dried leaf litter or the barks of trees when you're out nature rambling. You might hit upon a treasure trove!

Everybody loves a ladybird

Among the beetle clan this is an all-time favourite, particularly with children. They're small (up to 1 cm) rotund little beetles, generally bright orange, black and white with polka-dotted faces. There are around 5000 species and they live for usually between one and two years.

Apart from children, farmers and gardeners too love them because they feast royally on aphids and thrips—insects which are ruinous to plants. They have been used for biological pest control, and you can even buy packets of them at nurseries! But sometimes ladybirds can be pests too. They are largely carnivorous and are themselves (despite their bright warning colours) eaten by spiders, birds, frogs and dragonflies. In winter they hibernate together in huge numbers, and have even been found tucked away in their thousands in snow drifts up in the mountains.

Alas, it seems that they're not the sweetie little beetles we make them out to be, at home in picture-books and nursery rhymes and fairy tales! They have a dark side too.

Partners are not particularly faithful to each other and their larvae may even cannibalize adults! That's like a thirteen-year-old eating an aunty or uncle. A ladybird lays her eggs near a potential colony of aphids so her larvae have plenty to eat. Another lady arriving at the spot with a similar idea will sniff out the larvae and will flee because she knows they may well turn on her and gobble her up too! Ah then, we all have our sinister secrets…

The bratta-tat-tat bombardier beetles

The 500 or so varieties of these ground beetles are armed and dangerous though unlike us they use their guns only for defence. But slung under their abdomens are their 'machine guns' which they can swivel around pretty widely to line up accurately and nail their victims. If there's a threat they let loose with a burst of staccato shots (which make a popping sound) firing small jets of boiling, toxic spray at their targets as many as twenty times in succession, usually enough to take down the enemy.

Inside their abdomen they store their dangerous blast-producing chemicals in separate chambers. One chemical is hydrogen peroxide, which all of us have (and which is used to bleach ladies' moustaches) and the other, a group of chemicals called hydroquinones (beetles use quinones to harden their elytra). When these are mixed with the help of a triggering agent in a specially toughened chamber, all hell breaks loose! The hydrogen peroxide breaks down into oxygen and boiling water and the hydroquinone mixes with the oxygen to form highly corrosive benzoquinone.

Hot and volatile, this explodes out of the bombardier beetle's backside in a series of blasts, leaving its gun barrel smoking and the victim staggering, stunned or dead! The gun turret can swivel freely, rather like a swashbuckling Schwarzenegger firing his gun, even firing over the beetle's 'shoulders', though it cannot point directly at the beetle's own head, which would be disastrous.

Bombardiers are found everywhere except Antarctica and are carnivorous. It's believed they developed this technique to enable them to escape from attacks by wasps and ants. It generally takes the beetle precious long seconds to unfurl its wings from under its elytra in order to escape when attacked, and by machine-gunning the enemy in the meanwhile it buys itself enough time to do so and fly away. Now how many times have we seen this stunt used in the movies?

Fireflies: Emeralds in the dark

The rain had stopped and all you could hear now was the soft plink-plonk of raindrops falling off the gleaming leaves. The night was velvet black. Suddenly, you started…what was that? A tiny green light wafting weightlessly between the trunks of the pine trees, winking on and off…Have you had too much to drink? But no, now there seemed to be a flotilla of winking emeralds floating wave-like through the trees. From the undergrowth more lights winked on and off. Some of the floaters headed straight for the patio (possibly hypnotized by the lights) and landed on the wall, their green lights still pulsing. What were they: nano-spaceships from Mars?

Fireflies! Or lightning bugs! Glow worms! Ironically, they are neither flies, nor bugs nor worms. They're soft-bodied beetles, all 2000 or so varieties of them. They haunt temperate and tropical lands, preferring damp wooded areas and marshes, and in India are most prominently seen during the monsoons. There are a lot of accounts of good studious children capturing them in jam jars and using their light to do their homework, in places where there's no electricity. They really make a magical sight when hundreds sail through the dark, their movements serene and wave like.

So how and why do these ethereal insects perform their magic? Well, like the bombardier beetle (but not involving any violence at all) the lovely green light is produced by the mixing of chemicals and enzymes in the beetle's lower abdomen. It's a cold light, producing virtually no heat at all. A chemical called luciferin is mixed with an enzyme called luciferase in the presence of magnesium ions, oxygen and a power-producing compound called ATP (Adenosine triphosphate) which all of us have and which powers our cells and muscles. The lovely emerald light is produced as a result and the firefly can switch it on and off at will.

What's the purpose of this lovely display? Well, the fireflies wafting through the trees are guys out on date night looking for girls. The girls hang around in the undergrowth and if they see winkers that impress them they wink back— and the date is set! Each species of firefly has its own coded wink, so they don't land up with the wrong kind of partner!

But the lady of one species of firefly, the Photuris, is a real femme fatale and plays a dirty game. She lies in wait on the leaves and flashes a 'come hither' signal belonging to a different species: Photinus. Seduced, the gullible Photinus dude lands eagerly on the leaf, looking forward to a night of making out. Alas, he gets eaten by the lady instead and becomes dinner and not the date!

It's said that the lady behaves in this reprehensible way because the Photinus dude possesses toxic chemicals which she doesn't have, and which she needs to pass onto her larvae.

Firefly larvae live on the ground as grubs for as many as two years and are ferocious hunters of slugs, snails and earthworms. Fireflies themselves are hunted by frogs, some of which stuff themselves with so many that they begin glowing themselves!

Sadly, firefly populations around the world seem to be falling. The culprits here are habitat destruction, the indiscriminate use of pesticides and increasing light pollution. Like all romantics, fireflies like velvet dark nights. Forests in South East Asia (a favourite haunt) are being cut down at a criminal rate, and the light from towns and streets confuse and dazzle them, ruining their date nights. In some countries like South Korea and Mexico, they have become a draw for tourism and are caught by the million for certain festivals and then released often in unsuitable habitats. As many as 17 million were said to be caught in China in 2016.

Blister beetles: 'Blistered be thy tongue!'

This is what Juliet snapped at her nurse when the lady spoke ill of her precious Romeo! And surely, if there had been a blister beetle on Nurse's tongue it would indeed have blistered!

In India, blister beetles which generally appear during and after the monsoon, are usually large black and red insects which fly with a loud buzzing sound, weaving erratically around as they take off. Worldwide estimates vary between 2250 and 7500 species (which seems to mean we really don't know how many there are), of which around 107 are found in India. Here I've noticed they seem to have a great liking for anything, particularly flowers, which are mauve or yellow or orange. So maybe it'll be wise not to wear those colours in their presence.

Get on the wrong side of a blister beetle and it will indeed blister you! If irritated, it will exude a yellow liquid, a toxic chemical called cantharidin, on your skin and cause blistering. But I once watched a gang of black ants (the same kind which had taken apart a huge carpenter bee) get after a blister beetle, which sure enough produced its toxic yellow liquid. It didn't seem to affect the ants at all. They just continued to harry it until in disgust it took off from the bloom it was on. Blister beetles are not regarded kindly by farmers or gardeners.

Blister beetles lay between 3000 and 4000 eggs and their larvae are parasites of bees and grasshopper eggs. I always enjoy watching the adults take off. It's a laborious process: first they open up their elytra over their shoulders, then clumsily unfurl their crumpled black wings, rev up their engines and take off in a wobbly way, rather like a helicopter trying to get airborne in a playful wind with an inexperienced pilot at the controls!

The Whirligigs: Dodgem beetles

Whirligig beetles always remind me of those dodgem cars kids have so much fun with at fun fairs where you spin around banging into one another. Actually, whirligig beetles would be extremely offended by this comparison, because unlike dodgem cars they never actually bump into each other while gyrating madly on the surface of a still pond or water body.

They belong to a family of water beetles and are well equipped for this lifestyle: they are small, hard and oval shaped, their elytra are water repellent, and they can see both under and above the water thanks to 'divided' eyes. When alarmed they swim underwater and may exude a smelly liquid that drives predators off. They feed on insects that drop into the water and the female lays her eggs underwater in rows.

It's always entertaining watching a cluster of these beetles whiz, whirl and gyrate on the water spinning madly but never once colliding. It's thought they use the tiny ripples formed by the waves they generate due to their swimming motion as a form of radar to avoid banging into one another. Worldwide it's thought there are 700 species of whirligigs around, spinning around giddily in ponds and calm streams.

Darkling beetles: Fog drinkers

These beetles, also known as fogland beetles, live in the sizzling arid Namib Desert in South Africa where temperatures may reach 50 degrees Celsius and it very rarely rains. So, as any survivalist will tell you, 'hydration' is a problem.

The darkling (or fogland) beetle, a fairly long-legged, flat-backed beetle that has made the Namib its home has solved its drinking problem by conjuring up water from fog and moisture in the air. Every morning, when it is still cool and the fog rolls in from the ocean, the beetle scurries up a dune or ridge and facing the wind, raises its bottom, head facing down, its body angled at 45 degrees. Its hardened wings unfurl widely and catch the tiny droplets of fog. These droplets squat low thanks to the water-attracting qualities of the wings, other little droplets joining them until they're too big and heavy and roll into the rough troughs on the wings, which are waxy and water repellent. The large drop now just rolls down the trough like a bead of mercury into the mouth of the grateful beetle which can drink its fill. We are now using this same technology to design self-filling flasks, which could be invaluable for trekkers going to such arid places.

I was standing next to a kumquat bush, watching a lime butterfly hover around it, in the hope that it would land and lay its eggs on the underside of a leaf, when a movement caught the corner of my eye. I turned and had a look: oh, oh, what I had assumed to be a rather large elongated leaf was weaving back and forth slowly as if rocked by a gentle breeze. And it was no leaf! It was emerald green, and had an evil triangular chinless face, studded with two enormous pea green eyes. It had assumed a posture of beseeching supplication, with its arms held out like a beggar asking for alms. But those arms were barbed with interlocking gin-trap spikes and those eyes moved relentlessly. It was one of the terrors of the insect world: a praying mantis.

Even as I watched, a furry bee hummed close. The arms snapped out and snatched it, the gin-trap arms closing mercilessly over the insect! Immediately, the head bent low and the mantis chomped off its victim's head and then proceeded to eat it the way you'd eat a bhutta. Tiny flies hovered foolishly in front of its eyes, but the mantis ignored them, focusing on its meal. At last it was done and dropped the dry husk of the bee and then wham! One of the flies just became dessert!

There are about 2400 species of praying mantis in the world of which around 200 are found in India. Generally they prefer warm, temperate and tropical habitats and are usually clad in leaf greens or bark browns. Some are dead ringers for orchids and flowers, so foolish bees and flies fly straight into those terrible barbed arms in the hope of getting nectar and pollen. They're related to termites and cockroaches and their earliest fossils date between 146 and 166 million years back.

Between half an inch and twelve inches long, they are ferocious predators. The ladies (of several species) have got themselves a fearsome reputation. They can't fly so they hang around on leaves wafting their 'come hither' pheromones in the air till a gentleman, usually smaller and who can fly, comes by. The gentleman is careful as he can be, and manages to get on to her back, clasping her lovingly. She in turn, will rotate her head and chomp his head right off even as his nether end continues to frantically do its duty. Some (ghoulish) scientists maintain that being suddenly headless enables the lower half to really freak out thus ensuring better fertilization of the lady's eggs because it is no longer connected to the part of the brain which regulates self-control. Other more sympathetic scientists say that this sort of cannibalism is usually only seen in mantises that are kept in captivity, that are being ogled at in their most private moments by paparazzi scientists giving themselves cheap thrills. It makes the lady real nervous so she chomps off her partner's head (comfort food?)! Also, they maintain that only poorly nourished lady mantises go in for this sort of thing. Well-fed (captive) Chinese mantises indulge in elaborate courtship dances before getting together. Yet another theory maintains that the lady does this so that she stocks up on (her late partner's) protein, which is good for the quality of her eggs. A mating session may last up to three hours, though if the lady is feeding on her husband all the while, there's probably very little of him left at the end of the honeymoon.

At any rate, if the shotgun wedding is successful, the lady will lay between ten and five hundred eggs in a frothy white case adhered to leaves or foliage that looks like a Styrofoam bag. The babies, which are called nymphs, are tiny replicas of their parents—and their first meal may be their very own brothers and sisters. Even mom may indulge in a baby buffet if she's still around. Needless to say, very few nymphs survive this baptism by cannibalism!

The mantis is well-equipped for hunting. Besides its gin-trap arms, it has huge stereoscopic eyes with a specialized area called the fovea which enables it to closely focus on and track movement from as many as 60 feet away and can leap with speed and precision. It is also able to rotate its head 180 degrees and look at you over its shoulder. Its movements are lightning fast, twice as fast as a housefly's. Apart from insects, frogs and lizards, it may even go for small birds. While mantises have been videoed grabbing hummingbirds coming to feeders, it has been maintained that this is unlikely to happen in the wild. But one list of the birds on the mantis' menu included warblers, sunbirds, honeyeaters, flycatchers, vireos and European robins! One species from Karnataka has even been observed fishing in small ponds!

Mantises are themselves sought after by birds, lizards and particularly bats. Some have developed a hollow chamber in their abdomen which somehow enables them to detect the bats' ultrasonic echo-locating squeaks and so take evasive action.

These charismatic cannibals have naturally caught our imagination, and have been kept as pets for eons. There are Chinese kung-fu fighting techniques based on the mantis' movements, and the word mantis comes from the Greek 'mantikos' meaning soothsayer or prophet, which is what the mantis' typical pose resembles. Ancient people accorded them supernatural powers. Even we are developing robots inspired by the mantis' powerful gripping forelegs so robots can climb steps, walk and grasp objects. But as one scientist mentioned, we should thank our stars that mantises are not as big as we are. We'd be in real trouble then!

Dragons from the Deep

(Dragonflies and Damselflies)

Believe it or not, dragonflies and damselflies are actually born underwater and will spend more of their lives (two to three years, sometimes more) prowling around at the bottom of ponds and streams terrorizing tadpoles and small fishes, than they'll do in the skies as adults, which is usually for just around a month. You see, their moms lay their eggs underwater on a submerged leaf or stalk. What hatches from these are fondly called 'nymphs' or 'naiads' though whoever thought of this must have probably been sniffing glue. What emerge are monstrous little grubs armed with terrible grappling hook jaws that whip out, grab and impale a victim and draw it back into the mouth in less than a blink of an eye. They skulk around the bottom of ponds and streams, breathing through gills in their bottoms and can move hellishly fast by giving themselves jet-propelled enemas! Here, their reign of terror may last two or three years and then finally, after molting several times as they get bigger, they make for the surface of the waterbody. Before dawn one morning, they'll find a stalk and begin crawling up it, into the open air for the first time ever. They find a suitable place to hang out and shed their skins one last time...

Pale, colourless and gleaming wet, the dragonfly (or damselfly) finally emerges. When I first saw one of these, I had no idea what it was. Then the colour slowly seeped into its enormous eyes, the wings straightened out and stiffened and I knew I was looking at a brand new dragonfly.

These guys have been around a long, long time—300 million years. One fossil unearthed in France had a wingspan of 70 cm or two and a half feet! Apart from getting smaller, their design has remained largely unchanged for 150 million years. They're thought to be the first insects to be able to fly and there are around 5000 species worldwide, of which 500 can be found in India.

They're aerial predators par excellence and can touch 90 kmph while chasing a victim. Other insects, like butterflies and other flies, as well as their own kind, are taken on the wing and consumed in mid-air. They'll engage in fierce dogfights with each other for rights to aerial corridors. And they're as well equipped as any warplane!

Their cellophane-like wings, often so beautifully stained and tinted, are strong and flexible, twisting and turning on their axes and enabling the insect to change direction and fly in any direction, even backwards. The mighty flight muscles have an automatic 'on' 'off' system: the moment the legs leave a perch, they'll begin beating. While at rest, dragonflies' wings lie perpendicular to their bodies, while those of damselflies are folded alongside their fuselages. For weaponry, they have strong biting mandibles and six strong spiky legs (useless for walking) forming a barbed basket into which the prey is scooped before the dragonfly bites down on it. The shock of whamming at 90 kmph into a victim is absorbed by body segments specially aligned to do this. Prey is sighted with the help of those two enormous compound eyes (they have three 'simple' eyes too), each equipped with around 30,000 lenses. God forbid, they have to change contact lenses every morning! They can make out shapes and track movements and are able to turn their necks, heads and eyes in nearly any direction. They are gluttons, but burn a lot of calories, and can eat their body weight in food in half an hour. One champion dispatched forty flies in two hours!

They're not the sweetest romantics around. A 'gentleman' in search of a suitable lady will first transfer sperm from his nether end to a special sperm bag .in front of his abdomen. Then he'll spot a likely contender and hover rudely in front of her. Without so much as a by your leave, he'll roughly grab her by the scruff of her neck, often causing injury, with special claspers located at the tip of his abdomen and fly off with her, hitched on to him in tandem. Then she curls her own abdomen tip into his sperm bag, completing the lovely 'daisy chain' formation. Now suddenly 'gallant' he'll follow her down to the water or any shiny surface like the tarmac, or even underwater while she finds a suitable place to lay her eggs. His motive is probably to ensure there's no hanky panky in the meantime and that she'll have only his babies.

It's easy to tell the difference between the dragons and the damsels. Dragonflies are usually larger and more robust and can be seen flying high, even over treetops. Damselflies are much smaller and drift close to the ground, especially over ponds and water bodies.

These fierce predators have plenty of enemies. The nymphs are taken by big fish, and birds hunt the adults relentlessly. We, too, crispy fry them…

For long they've both fascinated and terrified us. In the past they've been called the 'devil's darning needles' and were accused of sewing up the mouths of little children. Actually children have often been cruel to them: catching them and tethering them and then flying them like kites! Dragonflies were also called 'horse stingers' because they were often found hovering around the animals. They were after the horseflies which pestered the animals. Dragonflies neither bite nor sting and can be great pest controllers, taking down large numbers of flies and mosquitoes. Their presence or absence around a water body is often an indication of how polluted it is: some dragons only like clean water, others seem okay with the murky stuff.

In India, the best time to look out for dragonflies is before and after the monsoon. With their lovely colours—pillar box red, gold, black, jade green, electric blue, and magenta etc, they can be as attractive to watch as birds. We've finally begun giving these insects the attention they're due and some cities even hold annual 'Dragonfly Festivals,' popularizing them. But be warned: dragonflies are fearless! Intrude on one's airspace and you will be relentlessly charged and challenged and seen off the property!

Watch a butterfly traipse erratically through the sky and you'll be convinced it should be booked for drunken flying. Can it even see where it's going as it jerks this way and that in every which way? But then it approaches a flower and hey presto, lands with all the precision of a helicopter pilot putting down on a postage stamp! That's just one of the many little tricks and miracles this remarkable insect has up its sleeve. It is of course, one of the most popular insects in the world because of the kaleidoscopic colours and patterns on its wings. There are plenty of varieties to choose from: 18,500 species or so, found worldwide (except Antarctica) of which 1400 are found in India. Fossils date back to 56 million years ago, though the earliest fossil of a moth, their night-flying partying cousins, stretches back 190 million years.

At any rate, they have the most astonishing life cycle. They hatch out of eggs—some pearl-like, some beautifully ridged and patterned—between 100 and 200 of which are laid singly or in groups depending on the species. But they're all laid on a particular food plant. Their moms know only too well that the caterpillars that hatch from the eggs will be extremely fussy eaters and refuse every other type of leaf. When they hatch, the caterpillars will first eat their eggshells so as not to waste any protein. Then they'll begin their life of gluttony, consuming leaf after leaf of their food plant with the help of strong jaws. The chewed-up leaf is processed in its large tube-like intestine and then stored as a layer of fat in what is called, you guessed it, the 'fat body'! Often caterpillars work their way around the areas of the leaf where the most toxins are, and some will even imbibe the toxins for later use. To escape the unwanted attention of birds and lizards, some will disguise themselves ingeniously as bird droppings (which bird will want to be caught eating its own droppings!?) or simply camouflage itself like a fallen leaf perhaps. Many feed at night and during the day lie doggo along the midrib of the leaf to merge with it completely. Their droppings, called frass, are shot away as far as possible from them so as not to give the game away. If by chance they face an unpleasant encounter, some will rear up and hiss, and from two protrusions on their heads which are sometimes red and bloody looking, will pretend to be a snake or let out a stink putting the attacker off. Many species of caterpillars are gaudily coloured and striped, warning predators that they are toxic, or are armed with spines and fine hairs that sting and itch. Most caterpillars can also spin silk (it always reminds me of a magician pulling ribbons out of his or her mouth), and some will group together in their thousands and spin huge silken tents over trees (they are called tent caterpillars) under which they live safely.

If you spend your life only eating and sleeping it's obvious that you are going to put on weight, which the caterpillar does—and how! And it's also clear that you're not going to be able to fit into your clothes for very long. The caterpillar has a simple solution: every now and then (maybe four or five times in its caterpillar avatar) it discards its old outfit under which a brand new outfit has been growing. After four or five such changes during which it has grown grossly, the caterpillar appears to have a complete change of heart. Like a Sumo wrestler deciding to atone for his past gluttony, it decides to go on a fast! It might even leave its beloved food plant and go off to find a quiet twig or branch. Here it sticks a pad of silk and attaches itself to it and hangs head down, and will remain thus twitching occasionally if disturbed, for maybe ten days to a fortnight. Some species, not liking this hang-down-your-head posture, spin a silk sling like a hammock, so they're face up. It strips itself of its last caterpillar outfit, and underneath, a chrysalis, a tough shell-like covering, lies waiting to be revealed. Inside the chrysalis a miracle begins unfolding.

It is fascinating trying to piece together how exactly this miracle takes place. Scientists have used what they called 'micro-CT scanning' to see what goes on inside the pupa as it develops. Actually, the process begins as soon as the butterfly's egg hatches. Apart from 'normal' cells which form the muscles, gut and other parts of the caterpillar, there are bundles of almost secret cells, called imaginal discs. Each disc, so called because they're disc shaped, has the blueprint of a particular part of the butterfly-to-be: thus there'll be two for the eyes, a pair for the wings, one for each leg and so on. Now as the caterpillar begins its gastronomic orgy, the normal cells begin getting bigger and bigger. But the development of the imaginal cells remains under 'lockdown' bathed in a juvenile hormone which stops their development. As the caterpillar gets too big for its skin, a molting hormone called ecdysone is released, which triggers the molting process. The juvenile hormone is meanwhile still putting the brakes on the development of the imaginal discs. The caterpillar sheds its skin around five times, each time spurred by a burst of ecdysone. When this happens for the last time, usually the fifth time, the levels of the juvenile hormone begin to drop. And hey presto, the imaginal discs swing into action and begin developing. Once the final molt is complete and the chrysalis is formed they really go in all guns blazing! Because now, other enzymes called capsases are released and these program the 'normal' caterpillar cells to self-destruct into their constituent protein parts into a sort of energy drink or nourishing soup. This provides the growing imaginal discs with the nourishment and energy they need to develop completely into various parts of the butterfly, a process that can take a fortnight or so. The process is called homometaboly, meaning 'complete metamorphoses', and of course butterflies are not the only insects that indulge in it.

It is really miraculous—and I've always believed that everyone should at least once see a newly-minted butterfly emerge from its chrysalis—it's a wondrous spectacle. This usually happens early in the morning, and yes, you'll be kept waiting! At last, the chrysalis twitches one last time and then splits open across its width. The freshly minted butterfly emerges tiredly like a canoeist climbing out of his kayak, and crawls to a nearby branch. Its wings are wet and crumpled, but its eyes large and lustrous. It'll hang down its wings, pumping fluid into their fretwork of veins, and spread them out to stiffen and dry. The wings are made up of extremely thin cellophane-like material called chitin, which is covered with layers of overlapping scales, wonderfully coloured and patterned rather in the manner of tiles on a roof. That is why when you handle a butterfly, you'll notice pollen-like dust on your fingers—those are the protective scales coming off the wing. It is vital that the wings hang down and dry properly if the butterfly is to fly: sometimes the butterfly gets stuck in the foliage, or has been attacked by a parasite and can't do this: Sadly it'll be crippled for the rest of its life.

Its watch-spring like proboscis, the drinking tube, comprises two parts when the butterfly emerges and it has to sort of clip them together to make one workable drinking tube. The clubbed antennae are used for smell and sensing air currents and the butterfly famously tastes with its feet.

After its past gluttony, the butterfly now swears on a liquid diet. Ah yes, you'll think, delicate sips of sweet nectar, how fitting for such an ethereal insect that reminds you of socialites at cocktail parties. Sure, and like socialites they also have a taste for blood, sweat, tears (even yours), alcohol, rotting meat, liquid mud and dung! But this is only because they obtain vital minerals and vitamins from these fermenting foodstuffs. You might have seen groups of butterflies hovering over a cowpat or elephant dung or mud puddle. Actually, this practice is delightfully called 'mud-puddling' and in some cases, apparently only the gents indulge in it. They'll suck up all the goodness from the dung and go off and offer it to their girlfriends and partners while honeymooning with them, so that she lays healthy eggs. But they are also the ultimate sugar freaks, and can detect the sweetness in a solution comprising one part of sugar and 300,000 parts of water.

Once its wings are stiff and strong, the butterfly takes to the skies usually in search of nectar and a mate. For a long time, aeronautical engineers were befuddled by butterflight (as well as the flight of most insects) as according to conventional 'steady state' aerodynamic theory the butterfly ought not to be able to create enough lift. Slow-motion photography revealed some of its secrets. It's really a very complex combination of things including the creation of tiny tornadoes which roll off the wings and vacuums created by the sudden opening of wings (called the 'clap wing', you can sometimes hear this in pigeons executing a take-off too) as well as the ability of wings to twist completely along their axis so as to help provide lift during both the upstroke and down stroke.

While it doesn't have the sharpest of eyes, a butterfly can make out the shapes and colours of flowers—and potential mates—which are also located by pheromones. It'll waft its own pheromones around a potential partner wooing her. Males of some species are boorish Casanovas, they'll hang around the chrysalis of a yet-to-emerge lady and pounce on her as soon as she does (sometimes they just go for it even when she's still in her boudoir so to speak). She, sensible lady, will store the male's sperm, often delivered in packets like an Amazon parcel I suppose, in a special sac called a bursa. She'll fertilize her eggs as and when she's ready to lay them.

Despite their warning colours and even the toxins they may store in their bodies, butterflies are preyed upon by birds, frogs, toads, lizards, spiders, wasps (which hideously anesthetize a caterpillar and then lay an egg on the supine creature) and other insects. Some, which are non-toxic, simply dress themselves up to look like their toxic cousins! They are also prey to fungal infections. Some sport 'owl' eyes on their wings, which they open suddenly to startle predators (rather like someone quietly creeping up to you and yelling 'Boo!') and others have false heads and tails so they have a 50:50 chance of escaping when attacked.

We too have a shameful history of 'collecting' them, killing them and displaying them in frames, or fashioning artworks out of their wings. Fortunately, butterfly collecting seems to be on the decline. In the past, butterflies were also often regarded as ill omens (in some cultures, the opposite was true) for absolutely no reason at all. One disgruntled entomologist and cockroach fan, the ex-curator of the Los Angeles Museum of Natural History, perhaps referring to their diet, unkindly called butterflies 'pretty cockroaches'. But these pretty cockroaches are useful pollinators. They can't carry as heavy a load of pollen as bees, but can take them over longer distances.

But make no mistake these flippant dilettantes are real toughies. Apparently you can put a butterfly in a glass jar, suck all the air out of it and then suddenly let the air back in, and the insect won't miss a heartbeat. Such a sudden change in pressure will kill us—and elephants too! These flimsy looking flyers are capable of the most astonishing migratory journeys. Easily the most publicized of these is the 3000 mile (4500 km) trip the famous monarch butterfly makes from its summering grounds in Canada and the northern United States to one small patch of mountainous forest in south-west and central Mexico. As the weather gets colder, and the days shorter, the monarchs set off in their millions, flying unerringly south or south-west depending where they started off from, using the sun and the earth's magnetic field to navigate. But they will never make the return trip. The spend the winter in warm Mexico, breed and die and their children begin the long haul back north as the weather warms up. But this generation will fly just a small part of the way, stopping, say, in lantana patches in Texas to breed and die. Their progeny will then resume the journey north (how they know that they just have to go and in which direction to fly boggles the mind) flying maybe hundred-odd miles before breeding again and dying: it may take four or five generations before the butterflies finally reach their summering grounds, to which they've never been before.

But the record for the longest migration is held by the painted lady butterfly, which makes a 9000 mile (14,500 km) round trip from Africa to the Arctic every year. Some Indian butterflies also go on marathon journeys during the monsoon. It's amazing how a flimsy creature like a butterfly can manage these monumental journeys, battling winds, air currents, storms et al. They have an efficient manner of flying, getting up there with the big boys like the vultures, flapping their wings and then gliding long distances to save energy.

If you think butterflies are the ultimate partying insects think again. Wait till you meet their dowdy, dumpy cousins the moths! These guys come out after dark to dance the night away in front of all the bright lights, scattering enticing 'come hither' perfumes into the night air. They may not have the most glamorous dress-sense, but boy can they boogey!

Silently they emerge after dusk, as darkness descends. They'll make for the nearest tubelight or lamp or fire and begin to dance dizzily around it. Usually, they're dressed in ethnic colours—dusky browns and beiges, jade greens, cream, red ochre, even gold and silver and the like, resembling folk dancers of an ancient past clad in raw silks. Tragically, most seem to have suicide on their minds because like kamikaze pilots, they spiral closer and closer to the hot source of light and then crash and burn. Moths have been fatally attracted to lights, or more accurately, fatally disoriented by them, since time immemorial and we're still arguing over why.

One popular but not universally accepted theory is that of 'celestial or transverse orientation'. As several species of moths are migratory, they need a compass to guide them, and they use the source of a far distant light from the moon and bright stars for the purpose. If they could fly such that they kept the angle between them and the light source constant, they could fly in a straight line. As the light source was so far away, it didn't really appear to shift, so this was easy. But when the light source chosen was closer, like that of a lamp or fire, that angle kept changing, and to correct that the moth had to change direction, leading it to spiral fatally right into the light source. There's evidence to show that migratory moths also have an internal geo-magnetic compass which helps them find their way.

Some scientists are not convinced. They maintain that all moths are not migratory so don't need the moon or stars to steer by; in fact as many as 70 per cent are non-migratory. Others maintain that the ultraviolet waves emitted by the light source attract moths. Many flowers have ultraviolet colours, which serve as a sort of guiding runaway lights for moths (and other insects). Seeing a whole host of these ultraviolet colours being emitted say by a bug zapper may fool the moths into thinking that a nectar feast awaits them in a bed of flowers!

Other scientists go the opposite way. They say that the infrared emissions from a light source resemble the sort of infrared waves coming off the pheromones of a lady moth, which seduces the gentlemen. (No mention of what lady moths do!)

Another question which bothered scientists was why moths remained near bright lights, in other words why are they ready to dance the night away! Like our eyes, the eyes of moths are loaded with light sensors which adjust according to the brightness of the light received by them. In brightly lit conditions, all of the thousands of sensors receive and adjust the light received by the thousands of individual lenses. In low light conditions, all the lenses channelize the light they receive to a single sensor, increasing its sensitivity. In moths, it takes a while for this to happen as they move from brightness to darkness and in that period they are temporarily blind and easily subject to predation. It's like what happens when you are suddenly subjected to a bright light after being in the dark and vice versa, you experience a momentary period of blindness, as your eye adjusts. Unfortunately, they don't seem to learn from this experience and will come again to the bright lights to spend the nights there.

And this can cost them their lives! Apart from the danger of crashing into the lights, another threat looms. In Kasauli, many years ago, I used to step out of our hotel room early every morning and check on the lovely moths on the wall outside dealing with their hangovers after having boogied the night away around the outside light. Promptly at around 6 a.m. a hungry breakfasting mob of tits, mynas and other small birds would turn up and systematically gobble up the resting moths.

But moths are remarkable insects in many ways. Firstly, they hugely outnumber butterflies as far as their species numbers go: some say up to 250,000 and counting. This is possibly because they were around and evolved much before butterflies did. Earliest fossils date back 190 million years. They maybe ethnically chic…um…dowdy according to some, but the ladies wear powerful perfumes which can draw the gents to them from as much as 11 km away. The Indian moon moth is one such. In addition, the gents flutter around them disseminating their own macho colognes! Some, like the tiger moths, are in fact strikingly colourful—their bright reds and yellows warn predators that they won't forget how foul (and toxic) they are if they take a bite. There are around 100 families of moths in India, from the gigantic silk moths to tiny feathery plume moths.

Their life cycle follows the same pattern as that of butterflies: egg, pupa, cocoon and adult, with the same miraculous changes occurring. The pupae of some moths go underground in order to pupate in peace and be safe. Unlike butterflies however, which just develop a chrysalis under their fat caterpillar skins and then shed their skin, moths spin their cocoons out of silk, some spinning lengths of silk 1.8 km long! Some larvae take an inordinately long time to become cocoons and then adults. The caterpillar of the Arctic wooly bear moth takes seven years to do so: it sort of shuts down during the harsh Arctic winters when temperatures can plummet to -70 degrees Celsius. As winter draws close, they begin to spend most of their time basking and the rest feeding and moving around. They molt once every year. Their life as an adult (emerging in summer) may last just twenty-four hours in which time they have to find a partner and mate. It's a tough life! It really is for some other caterpillars too, because if there's a food shortage, baby caterpillars will turn on each other and turn cannibal. If you remember, Hannibal Lecter in *The Silence of the Lambs* placed a dead Death's Head moth in the mouths of his victims to terrorize everyone. The poor moth only had a skull-like marking on its body! This moth actually emits squeaks, both in its caterpillar form and as a moth, when handled.

How do you tell a moth from a butterfly? By and large, moths are stubbier, hairier and unlike butterflies do not have clubbed antennae; theirs are straight or delicately feathery. By and large, moths hold their wings open wide while at rest, while butterflies fold them vertically over their bodies. I would not say that butterflies are more beautiful. They may be more colourful and glamorous but some moths display exemplary good taste in their outfits. And then of course, while all good butterflies go to bed before dark, moths come out to disco the nights away!

Make no mistake they have a hard time surviving, being seen as food by spiders, birds, geckos, bats et al. Some simply dress up like their predators—even as praying mantises and tarantulas—others load up with toxins and fiery colours (toxins imbibed when they were caterpillars). Some moths have learned to detect and even jam the echolocation system used by bats, diving out of the way at the last minute, or emitting their own ultrasonic squeaks to befuddle the bats! Moths with long kite's tails use the twisting and turning of the tail streamers, which are cumbersome to fly with, to deflect the ultrasonic squeaks coming from the bats and so confuse them. Many years ago, I was once sprayed with a hot acrid liquid by an outraged hawk moth I tried to photograph. I had to back away pretty hastily. Viewed side on, the gigantic Atlas moth (which can cover your palm) shows the profile of a striking snake's head on both its wing edges. Some moths have 'owl eyes' painted on their wings to scare off potential predators.

But it's as pupae that they suffer the most, being chock-a-block full of protein: 95 per cent of all nesting bird species shop avidly for caterpillars for their babies. Fat caterpillars are a major food item in many African countries. Horribly, we boil alive the cocoons of the silkworm moths to obtain silk from them; a multi-million-dollar enterprise, which upsets animal activists greatly. This is not done out of vindictiveness (though try explaining that to a moth): when the moth begins to emerge from the cocoon it emits a fluid which dissolves the silk so that it is able to do so. So we immerse the cocoon in boiling water to prevent this from happening and we can unravel the silk thread unbroken. To defend themselves, many caterpillars are armed with spikes and fine stinging hairs, which itch and burn like mad, though the fearsome looking wooly bear caterpillar only wears its furry coat to keep warm. (I still wouldn't stroke one.)

Well, the caterpillars of many species do manage to take some sort of revenge: they'll eat our clothes and blankets, defoliate entire forests and ravage crops on a mega scale. As adults, they have much the same appetite as butterflies, enjoying pollen, nectar, rotting meat, dung, mud, (all for mineral goodness), beer, rum and rotting fruit . But many moths do not eat at all as adults, and some, like the gorgeous Atlas moth and Luna moth, don't even have mouth parts, simply using up the energy they stored as pupae.

The largest moth, the magnificent Atlas moth of Southeast Asia has a nearly 1 foot (30 cm) wingspan, the littlest the *Stigmella maya* from Mexico is just 1.2 mm!

A moth also demonstrates clearly how evolution works. The peppered moths of England looked like the lichen and bark covering of a tree in England, merging perfectly, so they were hard to pick out while resting on them. Then came the Industrial Revolution and with it, mega clouds of smoke and soot covered the tree trunks and darkened them. And hey presto, soon enough the moths darkened too, now merging with the blackened trees. And when the soot pollution was cleaned up and the trees regained their normal colour, so did the moths!

Moths are important pollinators (the flowers that attract them use enticing perfumes rather than bright colours), one such being the hawk moths which are key pollinators for some Himalayan flowering plants.

Years ago, I used to step out into the garden after dusk every day to check out beautiful golden moths that used to come out and shimmer over the flowers. Other favourites were the delta-winged hawk moths some of which had lovely transparent wings and hummed over the flowers with their proboscis probing deeply, even in daylight.

Sadly, the number of moths one sees, especially in cities, seems to be falling thanks to light pollution. But if you're in a forest, it is always worthwhile hanging up a sheet outside with a bright light (a bulb will do) burning next to it. You'll be gobsmacked by the number and sheer variety of the moths that will cluster onto the cloth. In our brightly lit cities alas, we can only hope that when the nightblooming jasmine wafts its alluring perfume every evening, at least some of these wondrous creatures will grace the plants with their presence.

There you are, playing outdoors, kicking a football around, or simply lying back in the grass gazing at the clouds, when 'Owww!' you leap up with a shriek as something hums past your ears like a close-flying plane. You clutch your arm or leg or face, where you can see a small angry red spot begin to swell up. Yes, it's a childhood rite of passage—to be stung by a bee (or worse, wasp). Back home you watch tearfully or stoically (as the case may be) as a sterilized needle is used to remove the evil little stinger clinging tenaciously to your flesh. Every child has been, or should have been, stung at least once by a bee; though some children and adults really cannot take that risk because they can develop a life-threatening allergy to bee venom and would need an immediate trip to the hospital.

But humans have been around bees and known about them since the times of the ancient Egyptians and Greeks and began 'domesticating' them for their delicious honey some 4500 years ago. We began robbing hives much before that: 15,000 years ago! Bees evolved from ferocious carnivorous wasp species about 160 million years ago side by side with flowering plants. It's believed that some of these wasps may have preyed on insects which ate nectar, and which made them sweet and gave them energy, so some wasps decided that hey, why not cut out the insects altogether and go straight for the motherlode—nectar-filled flowers! And so, over time they became vegans—and bees.

Apart from merely consuming nectar (for carbohydrates) and pollen (for protein), bees used them in different forms to bring up their larvae and build their hives. Thus, they concocted honey, beeswax, bee bread, propolis (a kind of adhesive used to fill gaps in the hive) and royal jelly. The last is specially enhanced with nutrients and produced by 'nurse' bees, and are reserved for princess larvae which are being groomed to be queens, and for queens. (Some argue that royal jelly is fed to all larvae regardless of sex or status.) Many people believe that royal jelly has remarkable medicinal qualities but this has not been scientifically proven. The largest bee, a leaf-cutting species, measures almost 4 cm. The smallest, a stingless worker species, less than 2 mm.

Of course, there's no such thing as a free lunch and bees pay back flowering plants by pollinating them as they go from one bloom to another. A bee may visit over one thousand flowers a day! This is hugely important for us: it's believed that one-third of all human food is pollinated by insects and mammals, the majority of it by bees. Some bees are specialists and will visit only a single species of flower and its closely related family members, and are called monolectic. Others only visit a few flowering species or the flowering family it hails from, and are called, oligoleges. Most are generalists, or polylectic, collecting honey and pollen indiscriminately from all kinds of flowers. Bees are estimated to produce twice or thrice as much honey as they require. Apart from nectar collection, beekeepers actually rent out hives (a very profitable business) to farmers for their pollination services.

As bee populations continue to fall around the world due to various reasons like pollution, indiscriminate use of pesticides, attack by parasites, habitat destruction and global warming, we are heading for serious trouble. The phenomenon of 'colony collapse' when entire colonies die or vanish, has become a major cause of worry. And as usual, we've been greedy: not satisfied with the quantity of honey European honeybees produced, we cross-bred them with a ferocious species of African honeybees way back in the 1950s. Alas, the resulting Africanized honeybees turned out to be no better at nectar gathering as their European counterparts—but were manic! They had very short, incandescent tempers; they chased down their victims for miles and stung them to death. And in 1957, they escaped from Brazil and headed northwards. They've reached some of the southern regions of the United States, and have since caused havoc, swarming into downtown areas and suchlike just because perhaps some motorist rudely blew his horn at them! They're still heading north—200 to 300 miles a year.

Bees in general are pretty well equipped to collect pollen: some, like bumblebees, are furry and fuzzy so that the pollen adheres to their hairy bodies, while others have special 'carry bags' attached to their legs, which they fill up with pollen. To defend themselves, they have stings, and many bees are brightly coloured to warn off predators.

Today, there are some 16,000 species of bees in the world found everywhere except of course in poor old Antarctica, of which as many as 90 per cent are solitary. These include our familiar shiny black carpenter bees that hum around flowers like little winged motors. They nest in holes in bamboo shafts, twigs, wooden poles and suchlike where the female lays a single egg and provisions it with pollen and seals it and then makes another. She never lives to see her babies.

Of course, it's the colony nesting honeybees that have monopolized most of our attention. A hive is a well-disciplined place, ruled by a queen who has the sole privilege of having babies. The hive is inhabited by the queen's daughters—the workers and nurses and defenders—and her sons, which are called drones, who are useless for everything except their sperm. The queen can control how many of each she wants: if she wants daughters, she'll allow her eggs to be fertilized by the drones, if she wants sons she just lays an unfertilized egg, which hatches into a real mama's boy! The drone has no father, but he does have a grandfather. He has no sons, but his daughters can have sons, which will be his grandsons! Thus, in a hive all the sister-drones (called super-sisters) are related to each other by 75 per cent (half from their mothers and a quarter by their fathers), and to their brothers by one-fourth. And the closer the degree of relatedness, the more altruistic is the behaviour. To ensure maximum nectar gathering, the queen emits chemicals which turn her daughters into willing and tireless workers ('busy as a bee') who are unable to have their own babies. The drones just hang around. In temperate countries they are kicked out of the hive in winter, when resources thin out! When the queen dies, her daughters will develop new queens by selecting suitable larvae kept in special cells which will be fed exclusively on royal jelly so that they hatch into fertile queens.

Now to a recent phenomenal discovery: Scientists have found (and actually recorded this) that when all the potential queens are ready to emerge from their cells, they begin quacking. Yes, they really do sound like ducks! This warns workers that they're ready to come out, so could they please be released. Then, one potential queen is released and rushes around the hive actually 'tooting' like a toy locomotive! This informs all the workers to hold their horses and not open up any more cells because the emergence of another potential queen would mean a battle to the death for supremacy. The tooting queen eventually takes off to found her own colony, followed by admiring drones and now the workers in the hive are free to release the next potential queen incumbent!

The aam janta larvae are of course kept in cattle class and fed on bee bread (according so some biologists), and hatch into workers. A queen rock bee for example, who wants to lay eggs will embark on a honeymoon 'flight' accompanied by a swarm of eager Romeo drones. She'll mate and then land and begin the process of developing a new colony, quickly having worker daughters do the work of hive-making and baby care. She'll mate with multiple males, maybe ten or twenty and each line of daughters will be just half-sisters having the same mom but different dads. This helps in genetic variety, lessening the danger of the entire colony falling prey to some parasite or infection. (Some sister-lines may be more resistant than others.)

Now why would a female worker give up her right to be a mama, when according to Darwin's theory of 'natural selection' each living entity and gene fights tooth and nail to be a part of the next generation? Well, if all of the worker sister-bees began fighting each other for the privilege of becoming queen bee, there'd be chaos in the hive and the larvae would be neglected and die. The queen cannot let that happen, so suppresses the maternal instinct in her worker daughters by issuing chemical instructions, which turns them into zombie nannies and slaves! The good of the hive comes before the good of an individual bee. In some cases, as this one, natural selection chooses the good of the group above that of the good of an individual.

And the sister-workers do take good care of the hive, even if the work is endless. A worker honeybee in her brief five- to six-week lifetime will collect just one-twelfth of a teaspoon of nectar, so you can imagine the amount of work that has gone into provisioning a hive with honey. If it gets too hot inside, they'll cluster around the entrance and beat their wings, allowing air to circulate and cool things down.

Also, the hive and the queen have to be defended at all costs. If a vicious giant hornet turns up with the intent of later bringing its own forces to kill and eat all the bees and larvae, they will just pile on to it en mass, beating their wings and so make it overheat till it dies. If they have to die in defence of their hive, they will. But once a bee stings something, it is itself doomed. The poisonous stinger, embedded in the victim is attached to the intestines and muscles and nerves of the bee and can't be pulled out. As the bee pulls free it suffers from massive internal rupture and dies as a result.

Sometimes, however, 'cuckoo' bee species take advantage of colony nesting bees. They don't build nests of their own but will sneak into one, pretending to be a resident and lay their eggs in them. Their larvae will happily be fed by the authentic worker bees. The bee will feed on their larvae after they hatch into ladies armed with formidable stings! It's believed that as many as 10 per cent of bee species behave in this disgraceful manner. Bees have other enemies too: insects like praying mantises, spiders, and a host of birds from bee-eaters to honey buzzards, animals such as the honey badger and of course bears which can total a hive in no time at all. Then there's us with our poisonous chemicals and greed for more. Fortunately, most honey collectors (such as in the Sunderbans) have the good sense of leaving hives they've raided with enough honey for the bees to sustain themselves on.

Perhaps the most fascinating aspect of nectar collecting is the famous 'waggle dance' that foraging bees do after returning to their hives with good news. They dance in a strange figure-of-eight manner, by inclining themselves according to the angle of the sun with that of the nectar source they have found, the time for each waggle indicating the distance from the hive. They waggle at an angle then return to the starting point, first from the right then the left and waggle back up to the top of the 'run'. They may do as many as 100 waggle runs! Chemical signals indicate what kinds of flowering plants they have found. There are actually two (and a bit) forms of the dance; the round dance, done when the nectar source is nearby, say 10 metres away, then the 'transitional' dances (when the resource is 20 to 30 metres away) and the waggle dance proper when it is more than 40 metres away. It is believed that the waggle dance evolved from simple excitement over the finding of a prospective new nesting site, which spilled over into the advertising of a rich source of nectar. When a foraging bee found what it thought was a motherlode of nectar, it hotfooted back to the hive and danced out of sheer excitement, thus infecting the others, which followed it back to the source. But apparently, in spite of being ruled by a queen and being very disciplined, bees believe in democracy. A bee returning with news of a find is not believed straight away. A party of scouts from the hive head for the find and only if at least fifteen of them (which is the quorum) agree that it is worthwhile, will the rest of the workers head for it. If two or more foragers find different likely sites and return excitedly, they might even start fighting each other over whose site is better! By sending out a scouting party to decide, a more democratic decision is taken. We ought to follow their example in our decision-making too. Only different people have different, and often conflicting goals, while bees have only one goal on their minds: nectar and pollen.

The waggle dance has been criticized for several reasons: Some believe that bees in the hive may not correctly interpret the dance and so pinpoint the resource. Some dodo bees may not get the message even when the discoverer frantically waggles as many as fifty times, while some smartypants will know where to go with just five waggles! The thinking is that the amount of energy expended by the bees in decoding a waggle dance may be more than that required to forage for a source of nectar they remembered, so they make the more energy efficient choice. Apparently, studies have shown that in most cases up to over 90 per cent of the bees simply ignored the directions and headed for earlier discovered sources. Another view suggests that bees simply sniff the initial forager for perfume and head in the direction from which they get a similar scent!

A waggle dance may simply incite the bees to go foraging in whichever direction they wish. In temperate countries, there was usually no shortage of flowering plants to forage from, so the bees didn't really need to be instructed where to go. In tropical countries, like India, when trees in a forest come into flower in a particular season, it might be more useful if the bees were directed as to where these trees were in the forest, making the waggle dance more useful. Like languages, even waggle dances have their dialects and what's amazing is that bees from one locality can learn the waggle dance dialect of bees from another locality if they move there.

I've always felt bad when I've seen beekeepers clad in head-to-toe bee suits (though some from poorer regions of the world just cover their faces with cloth) remove massive combs from a hive after stupefying the bees with smoke. It really seems like daylight robbery! One can only hope that bees do indeed produce two or three times as much nectar as they need, so won't mind us helping ourselves to some of it. Some farmers in rural India who live near forests have found another use for bees: they string up a series of beehives, all linked to one another along the borders of their farms and fields. When elephants come looking for sugarcane or other crops, (they can destroy an entire crop in a single night) they disturb the hives, awakening the bees to fury. Huge as they are, elephants don't like being stung and beat a hasty retreat. As a bonus, the farmer is also able to harvest the honey.

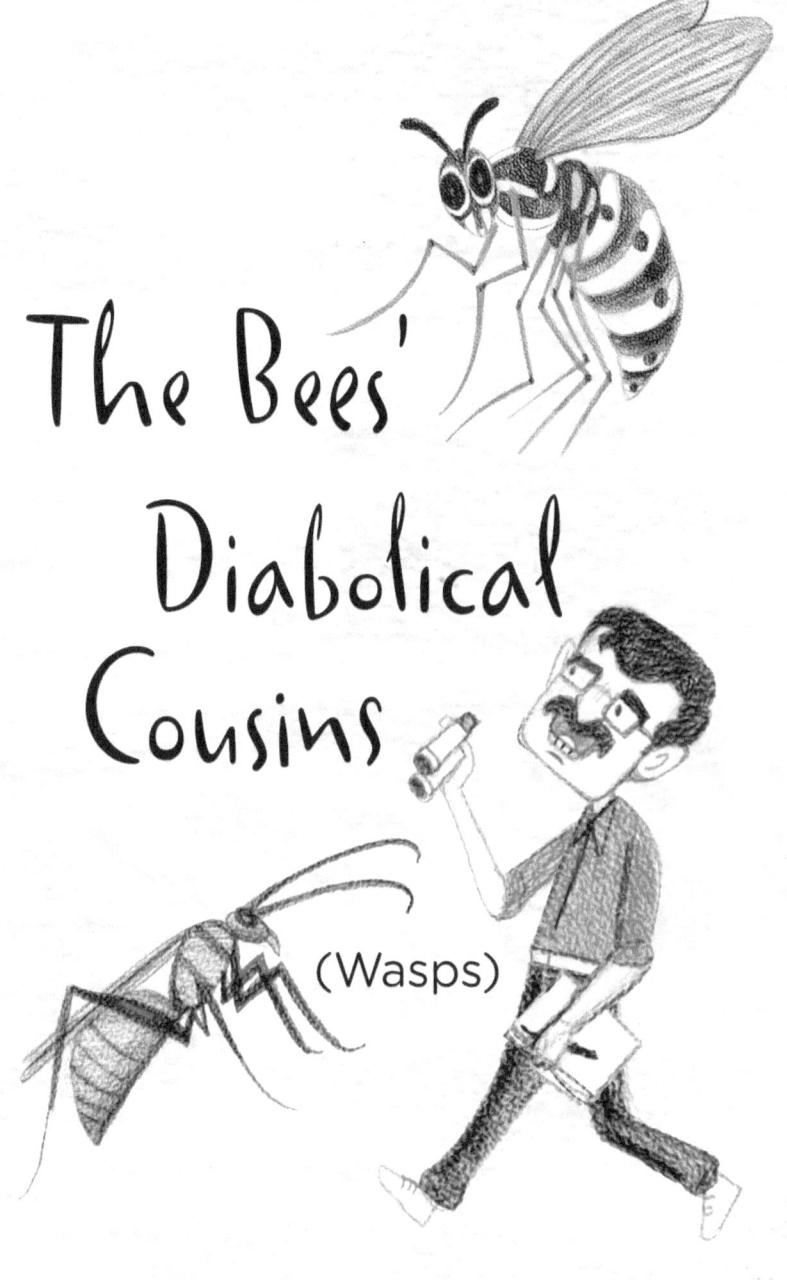

The Bees' Diabolical Cousins

(Wasps)

If you see a wasp winging towards you, you will instinctively duck out of its way. Sometimes alas, even that cannot be enough. Cooling off in the pool one summer, I noted that several orange wasps had decided to do the same and would land on the water, feet splayed out. Then one decided that the back of my neck was a good place to sunbathe from—and the damn thing stung me! It took a good forty-five minutes for the pain to subside and I've eyed these wasps warily ever since. Unlike bees, wasps do not leave their stings inside you because their stingers are smooth and not barbed. They can be withdrawn after giving you a venomous injection and then used to sting again! Be warned: do not antagonize one; wasps have notoriously short tempers and if you upset one, it will release a battle-cry pheromone which will summon the rest of the colony and then you'll be in real trouble.

Wasps themselves face trouble at the beaks of bee-eaters which are experts at sting and venom removal—they just bash the insect against a branch forcing the venom out. Honey-buzzards specialize in getting after one of the deadliest species of wasps: the Asian giant hornet.

It's easy to recognize a wasp (or a clever con-insect mimicking one). Firstly, they have the sort of metallic hard eyes that film-makers use for aliens and Martians: sometimes slightly slanted and blank as a metallic shutter. Then they have their famously slim waists, really filamentous thin in many species. In some species you can see the sting—a sharp, fine needle at their nether end ready to do its deadly work. They may be variously coloured: from metallic blue-black-green, to dangerously striped in orange and black to plain orange. There may be anything between 30,000 to 100,000 species in the world, living everywhere except in the polar regions. Most are solitary, while a few live in colonies. Earliest fossils date back 200 million years and bees are their nectar-gathering cousins. They do feed on nectar and plant sap, but most are hunters, taking live prey (spiders, caterpillars and cicadas seem to be a favourite) which they suck dry for themselves and chew up into small pieces for their young. How they bring up their babies can be quite diabolical.

Some monsoons ago, I noticed these slim blue-black wasps zinging into my bedroom and heading for my boombox or a set of bookshelves. I observed one such as it flew in from the bougainvillea creeper outside. There seemed to be something in its jaws. It flew to the bookcase, paused, and then disappeared inside one of the empty screw slots at the side of the shelf. Eventually it emerged, washed its hands (so to speak) and was off again, only to return after a short while to repeat the performance. This time it paused at the entrance and I saw what it was holding: a tiny spider, which it then stung before vanishing inside. Eventually, it sealed up the entrance to the hole with what looked like white cement and zinged away. I looked it up and concluded that it must have been a species of spider wasp that specialized in hunting spiders.

After a few days, in the interests of science, I broke open the seal, and with a penknife drew out the contents of the nest onto a piece of paper. Eight or ten feebly moving stiff spiders tumbled out, waving their legs like zombies, but then my blood ran cold… On the back of one of them was a small, yellow maggot-like grub that moved, as if trying to find a more comfortable position. It was the wasp's baby. The mom had laid her egg on the anaesthetized spider and gone. The grub was now eating the zombie spider alive, leaving its vital organs for last! After it had finished with one, it would hump its way onto another. Its mom had ensured that it had an ample supply of fresh food: all the spiders were alive, so still fresh. Had she killed them, they would have rotted and been of no use.

There was a strange epilogue to a similar wasp nesting event. A few days after yet another nest had been sealed up—and not investigated by me—I saw a wasp approach the sealed nest. Ruthlessly, it broke open the seal and dragged out the contents, in this case the curled up body of a nearly ready-made wasp! It just dropped this and then began filling the now empty cavity with freshly anaesthetized spiders. I don't know if she was the original mom and if so, why did she behave like this? Had she forgotten she already had a baby growing inside it? Did sheer instinct rule her behaviour? Or was it a totally different lady wasp that broke open the nest?

Then, another thought struck me. That first monsoon when I observed the spider wasp, I checked my room thoroughly. There were at least eight nests in various cubby holes in the room, each stocked with perhaps ten dead spiders. That made eighty dead spiders in my room alone! There were at least seven suitable rooms in the house where wasps could find nesting holes. That made a total of 560 dead spiders in the house! There were hundred apartments in my complex and if you took the same figure (560) you ended up with 56000 dead spiders in all the houses. Taking all the exteriors into account, such as stairwells, porches, the building walls and terraces themselves, you could easily quintuple that figure, which gives us a total of 5X 56,000 = 280,000 dead spiders in the buildings alone. A massacre! And I haven't taken into account all the other suitable places these wasps might nest in, like the gardens and trees and bushes! Then I wondered, what if all these over a quarter million spiders had been allowed to live: they'd be demolishing the population of other insects such as bees. So this was obviously just a tiny part of the balance of Nature being maintained, and Mother Nature does everything on a magnum scale!

Solitary wasps generally nest in burrows underground, or cavities (as we have seen), and some are ferocious enough to give even tarantulas the chills! They sting them and drag them into their underground burrows where they lay their eggs on the supine creatures. The sting of the tarantula hawk wasp is excruciatingly painful to humans. Ironically, adult solitary wasps live mainly on nectar. Apart from stocking her baby's pantry, the mom takes no further interest in her brood. We find solitary wasps exceedingly useful as they take down an enormous range of insect pests, which would otherwise bedevil our crops and fruit trees. Some solitary wasps nest together in small groups, but each 'queen' looks after only its own offspring in its cell. Some of course will steal the food of others and in some cases they will even pull the 'cuckoo' con, laying their eggs in the nests of other wasps in the neighborhood (sometimes after removing the incumbent larvae).

Social wasps that nest in colonies behave differently. To build their nests, which may be made out of mud and saliva, or chewed-up rotting wood, plant fibre, sap and resin (which sort of becomes like papier-mâché) social wasps arrange them in clusters of hexagonal cells, inside each of which an egg is laid by the 'queen'. After mating during her nuptial flight, in spring she finds a suitable location on a wall or a twig or branch and begins building a colony. Initially, just a few eggs are laid and like in bees, the queen can decide how many sons and how many daughters she wants. (Sons hatch from unfertilized eggs). She personally feeds the larvae of this 'first generation' with chewed up insects she hunts. Once the larvae pupate, the queen begins laying more and more eggs, which are looked after and nourished by their working sisters who also take care of their queen. There may be 5000 members in a colony, so it's best not to disturb them!

In temperate countries, as winter approaches, these diligent workers begin stuffing some of the larvae in the cells with more goodies and more frequently. A genetic switch turns on and instead of developing into workers the super-fed larvae develop into princesses—potential queens. Winter kills off the colony, except for the strongest of the potential queens, who survive and in the following spring take off to find a consort and begin the whole cycle again. The queen has special 'kin recognition' software you could say (chemical signals actually), which prevents her from mating with her brothers. Interestingly, the larvae of many species of social wasps produce a large amount of salivary secretions which are rich in sugars and amino-acids that help in producing essential protein-building nutrients. These are unavailable to the adults, so they are lapped up eagerly by the adults—a unique case of babies feeding their parents! Social wasps feed on nectar as well as the sugary sap and juice from fruits, but also suck up the bodily fluids of their insect prey. There's something in the smell of apples and bananas that make social wasps run amuck so it's best to keep your distance from these fruits if you see wasps hovering around them.

Among the most dangerous species of social wasps have to be the hornets (22 species), of which the most ferocious and diabolical is the giant Asian hornet. A dreadful creature in yellow and black (its Japanese version is orange and black) it may be as much as 5.5 cm long. An Asian giant hornet can decapitate as many as forty honeybees in a minute and they actively seek out hives. Once a hive is found (and presumably the guards neutralized) the hornet sends out a 'come hither' pheromone, summoning the entire colony, which can make short work of the hive and its inhabitants. As we have seen in the earlier chapter on bees, honeybees have taken measures to see this doesn't happen. At considerable risk to themselves (and several are martyred) they just pile en masse on the terrible enemy and snuff it to death. They beat their wings over it heating it up to 40 degrees Celsius at which temperature it dies, cooked alive.

While wasps don't really match up to bees when it comes to pollination and nectar gathering or making honey (which, they don't), there is one unique family of solitary wasps whose pollinating services are absolutely invaluable. The family comprises the 1000 or so members of the fig wasp clan and each species is responsible for the pollination of one of the 1000 or so species of figs. Thus, every fig tree species has its own private species of fig wasp that pollinates it—no other species of fig wasp can do the job. If that wasp were to die off, so would the fig tree. But conversely, if the fig tree species were to die off, so would the wasp, of hunger, so it's a mutual relationship. And it's a pretty exclusive one at that.

The fig wasp story is really like an ongoing soap opera with enough twists and turns to make your jaw drop. We've all seen and eaten figs. Among the famous fig trees (the Ficus family) are the banyan and peepal, so we all know them. But here's the first 'believe it or not' fact. What seem to be the drupes or berries—the figs which birds so love—are not really 'fruits' at all. They are the flowers of the fig tree. Flowers that have been turned outside in! If we did time-lapse photography of the fig drupe, stretching back millions of years, we would see the 'drupe' slowly opening, revealing a massed pack of tiny flowers inside. Totally opened up it might resemble a sunflower, which also comprises of hundreds of tiny flowers. If we reversed the film, we'd see the open flowers gradually close up (like a fist being slowly clenched) into the fig we know today.

This tiny closed-up 'garden' comprises both male and female flowers and a host of miniscule insect pollinators—the fig wasps. The male flowers cluster on the outside or rim of the opened-up garden, the female flowers are on the inside. Fast forward these to the present and the garden of flowers slowly closes up on itself, leaving just an infinitesimal hole at the top. It's through this tiny hole, custom-designed for the wasp, that a lady fig wasp (too small to see properly with the naked eye), enters. The male flowers are now on the top of the 'drupe' and the female flowers remain at the bottom.

Now, let's check out how, typically, the life story begins. We'll start with the grub of the fig wasp, nestled in a seed capsule deep in the middle of a female fig flower at the bottom of the drupe, on which it feeds. If the grub develops into a male wasp, it behaves barbarously. It is a wingless little wimp that hardly looks like a wasp! It will bite its way into the capsules of female grubs and actually mate with the yet unborn females—how gross can you get? Then, deservedly, it dies.

The poor female, when she emerges, wriggles her way through the drupe garden to the top where the tiny hole beckons her. As she passes all the male fig flowers, she carefully and studiously fills up her pollen bags (which are rather like saddlebags) with the help of special brushes on her legs. Then she's out at last, sniffing the air for the scent of a suitable fig tree, whose female flowers are ready to receive her largesse. When she finds one, she will squeeze her way through the hole at the top of a fig, shedding her wings in the process and basically getting a good scrubbing because it's such a tight squeeze. But then, she's inside the dark garden and now punctiliously searches out the female flowers at the bottom of the drupe and delivers her load of pollen to every single one of them, thus fertilizing them.

But in some, not all of these flowers, she lays her eggs as well which develop into the grubs we started this story with, which feed on the developing seed. Then the poor lady crawls into a dark corner and dies.

The smart lady fig wasp knows that if she were to lay her eggs in all the female flowers in a drupe, the grubs would eat all of the seeds preventing the fig from reproducing at all, which would not be good. In some cases, apparently the fig tree itself shuts the gate to prevent all the seeds from being eaten. The female tries to deposit her egg at the bottom of the 'style' of the female flower (that thin stalk-like tube that sticks out of the middle of the flower) by her ovipositor, so the grub can survive on the flower's seed capsules nestled at the bottom. But in some female flowers, this 'style' is very long so the ovipositor of the wasp cannot reach it to deposit her egg. So she gives up and moves on till she finds a 'short-styled' flower. Another control method some fig trees use is that if all the female flowers of a drupe are burdened with fig wasp eggs and hence doomed, the fig tree gets rid of the entire drupe, as there's no point in nourishing them. And in the process naturally the wasp eggs too will die and not develop into grubs and adults.

In some species, after mating, the female wasps are helped to escape from the fig by a group of suddenly chivalrous gentlemen (who do not die after mating) who will industriously bite open the fig to let them out. Well, you could say that some lazy bum male could take the easy way out. He could mate with the females, and just lie back and let other gentlemen spend precious energy biting an escape hatch for the ladies. And in doing so, he'd have more energy than they would to have a good time with more ladies. In the long run however, this could backfire. If he did this, and his genes were passed on more than that of the other males, then gradually all his descendants would also tend to be lazy bums. Eventually a stage could be reached when all the males are lazy bums not willing to cut open an escape hatch for the ladies who then would not be able to fly off and lay eggs. So the males and their place in the world would come to an end!

But a counterpoint to this argument is that the male wasp is not able to think of what's going to happen in the 'long run'. He's only interested in the immediate future. So if it is in his interest to lie back and let the other idiots do the work then he will. So why doesn't he? One theory states that in a particular flower, most of the males are brothers, having similar genes. A male who digs an escape hatch for females, with whom he as well as his brothers have mated, will disperse genes to the next generation and the tradition of biting an escape hatch continues! The lazy bum's genes get overwhelmed and are swept away.

Believe it or not, this is just the tip of the iceberg! A lot more hera-pheri goes on—when for instance parasitic fig wasps enter the picture! For the time being however, I think the above tale is enough to make your head swirl, so we'll end it here.

But there's one message that comes through clearly: we have to be very careful about how we treat even the most insignificant of insects. It's well known that the banyan tree is a 'keystone' species in any forest. (It is also our 'national' tree.) Different trees produce their drupes at different times of the year, ensuring there is always enough for birds and animals to enjoy all through the year. If for example we killed off the species of fig wasp that pollinated the banyan tree, eventually the trees would all die off. This assured food supply would stop. Also, by dispersing the seeds far and wide, the birds and animals ensure the continued growth of the forest, which is good for all. But if there were no fig wasps around to do the job of pollinating in the first place, the forest would slowly die too as birds and herbivores would not find enough to eat, and then the carnivores would have nothing to hunt either.

But what I like best about the fig wasp drama is this: The tiny wasp makes pretty sure that no banyan tree can have a bloated ego! Such an enormous, weighty, important, magnificent tree is wholly dependent for its survival on a miniscule insignificant looking insect only visible with a magnifying lens! So if you ever think of yourself as small and insignificant, perish the thought! Sometimes it is the littlest things that really are the biggest and should be tooting the loudest!

A bug may be snug in a rug, but we're usually not very happy about any bugs in any rugs. Or, for that matter, anywhere. We seem to find them very annoying.

Bugs hail from an enormous clan and come in weird and varied shapes and sizes (between 1 and 90 mm long) and it is thought they evolved some 300 million years ago. Bugs come in two main types: the vegans and the carnivores, both of which have mouth parts custom-designed for their respective preferences. And if you thought the vegans were harmless, bhola-bhala types, think again! They can be devastating and do far more damage than their bloodthirsty carnivorous partners. Their piercing and sucking mouth parts can attack any part of a plant—its stems, leaves, roots, fruit, and even seeds—and suck the life juices out of them until the poor plant wilts and dies. The carnivores, which are in the minority, consist mainly of the much hated bedbugs and assassin bugs, some of which can be very nasty customers indeed, considering the kind of diseases they pass on.

As the vegans form the vast majority, we'll deal with them first. Eggs are usually laid on the plant that the bug is going to feast on, though baby bugs may prefer different parts of the plant than their parents. Babies are born as tiny replicas of their parents. If bugs attack plants in swarms (which they often do), they stunt them as they suck the nutrition out of them. Some, while attacking leaves and stems may inject venom too, so the plant dies, while others secrete large amounts of 'honeydew', which other insects love, as does a sooty black fungus, which covers the plant and kills it. Bugs may even transmit viruses, which again can devastate plants. One such is the aphid, also known as plant lice, and so hated by growers of roses. (It can be heart-breaking to see your resplendent rose plant crawling with these tiny creatures.) There may be seven generations of aphids born in a single year, each with a lifespan between two weeks and two months and each lady aphid can have 150 babies in her lifetime. They live in colonies and are protected by ants, in exchange for the 'honeydew' they produce.

Among the crops that get sucked dry by bugs are rice, paddy, maize, sugarcane, wheat, sorghum etc, so they're not exactly welcomed by us. Many specialize in what they attack: here in India, I've always been amazed at how hordes of orange and black 'cotton stainer' bugs suddenly swarm all over the burst open pods of cotton of the silk-cotton tree. You can imagine the damage such bugs do in the cotton fields.

Anyone who has been to a forest would have heard the typical background whistling sound produced by the cicadas; a sound that reminds you of tinnitus. Each species of cicada however, has its own special tone and tune though they all begin to sound off at the same time in a forest, as well as shut down! How they switch on and off with such precision remains a mystery. Cicadas are among the largest of bugs and love the warmer regions of the world. They may remain nymphs for long periods of time; one typically has a life cycle lasting seventeen years!

Plant-hoppers or leaf-hoppers come from a huge super-family of bugs and feed on a wide variety of plants. One lot looks like the prickles on a rose stem, or as if they're sporting bull horns. Usually, they're stouter than most of their ilk. They have an entertaining way of leaping from the plant when disturbed, which I can't resist making them do!

Amongst the most destructive—agriculturally speaking—are the leaf bugs or plant bugs, which belong to one of the biggest family of bugs. Many have a hunchbacked look about them and they pierce the plant tissue and suck the sap, weakening or killing the plant. Some are brightly coloured, others drab and some are even predatory, taking down small insects.

They are separate from the leaf-footed bugs which look like they've attached leaves to their legs! They too are agricultural pests, sucking sap and are also known as twig-wilters. They measure between 7 and 45 mm in length and may be oval or slender or elongated. Some are toughies, with well-muscled femurs (thigh bones) which may be armed with spikes. They too can raise one hell of a stink if offended or threatened!

Scale insects and mealy bugs form another interesting family of bugs. The former have two varieties: armoured scale insects and unarmoured scale insects. The armoured ones have a tough exterior and are usually dressed in browns and blacks. The latter are softies! Perhaps one of the most unique of this clan is the lac insect, which produces a resin on the plant it feeds on from which we make shellac. The resin comes off in flakes and is dissolved in alcohol and used to colour, finish and polish wood, and give a gloss to nail polish. Way back in history, the first 78 rpm records were made out of shellac, before it was replaced by vinyl. Shellac is in fact being replaced by synthetic substitutes in many other areas where it was originally used.

Shield bugs a.k.a. stink bugs can be both vegans and carnivorous. The vegans can be hugely damaging to crops. Shield bugs have large, flattish, oval backs which may be colourfully marked out, very often resembling a tribal warrior's shield. The striking multi-coloured patterns serve as a warning to predators. Some shield bugs may be a perfect match with the kind of leaf the plant they feed on. I once spotted one on a rosebush—and that too only because it moved. Shield bugs are also known as stink bugs because they can produce powerful disgusting odours from special stink glands located between their second and third pairs of legs if you mess with them.

They're not the only bugs that use this form of defence. Many species of broad-headed bugs use this and they're reputed to be stinkier! They also have brightly coloured abdomens which they hide under drably coloured wings, which they suddenly unfurl to startle a predator. They do have broad, even square heads, with slender bodies and filamentous legs and bulging, protruding eyes. They suck the nourishment out of seeds. There are about 300 members in this family and they're found in temperate and warmer places, inhabiting savannas, dry and arid areas and seashores.

We come now to the carnivores. Amongst them are the bugs which may 'kiss' us and suck our blood while we sleep. Assassin bugs come from another large family of bugs (with around 7000 family members) and are sturdily built, between 4 and 40 mm long, with painful bites and are found around the world. The most dangerous among these is the notorious 'kissing bug', which crawls out at night and 'kisses' us near our eyelids and around our lips, leaving telltale red marks. Some nefarious kissers come from South and Central America and can pass on the very unpleasant Chagas disease to us, which though treatable can cause inflammation and seriously affect vital parts of the body such as the heart. It's said to cause as many as 12,000 deaths per year.

But by and large assassin bugs are predators and hunt down other insects, including cockroaches and bedbugs. They stab their victims with their proboscis and inject toxic saliva containing enzymes which apart from killing them, liquefies the insides of the victim and digests it, and is then slurped up by the bug! Many kill insect pests for us and are actually being used as a form of biological pest control. The saliva of others have raised great interest as they work against human pathogens, so all in all it seems these bugs get an A grade!

Some predatory aquatic bugs live on or in water. Among these are the water striders which swagger around on the surface of ponds and lakes hunting down small animals that might have fallen in. They're separate from 'water boatmen' which occur in large numbers and feed on aquatic plants. One aquatic family has four giant members which take down small fish and tadpoles!

Finally we deal with the very unpleasant bedbug or 'khatmal'. This one crawls out of the nooks and crannies of our beds and furniture and walls in the dead of night and helps itself to our blood while we sleep. It has a mouth which is beak-like and armed with a saw with which it cuts open human skin, quickly injecting an anti-coagulant and painkillers, so you don't feel a thing. Then it starts sucking and normally your blood pressure is great enough to fill it up in three to five minutes, swelling it up and turning it dark reddish-brown. It's attracted by the carbon dioxide you breathe out and prefers to attack your face, neck and arms—any expanse of bare skin it can find. After it's done, it quickly retreats into hiding, with the whole operation not lasting more than twenty minutes. Now, it will not take in any more blood until it moults or completely digests what it's sucked up. If you squash it, it will raise a stink! Extremes of temperature do not affect bedbugs much; they can tolerate the cold up to -10 degrees Celsius and heat up to 45 degrees. Ideally, they like to feed every five to ten days, though they can go without a blood meal for a year. They're not hugely troubled by household pesticides either, so may be tough to get rid of. They like living together (safety in numbers) and a fertile lady can have as many as 500 babies in her lifetime.

Normally, the bite location swells up but does not turn red, though if a whole bunch of bedbugs have a party on you, you may find a row of red markings on the part of your body they've attacked. Interestingly, pathologists can recover DNA from the blood of the bedbug's victims for as long as ninety days after the victim has been bitten, which may be useful in forensic investigations. (It would be interesting to read a detective thriller based on this fact!) Bedbugs can't fly and are oval in shape and pretty unprepossessing. They are annoying, even disgusting but don't pass on any awful, malevolent disease to us, though you could be severely allergic to them. Best to avoid them in the first place, thoroughly checking any new place you're sleeping in—like a decrepit rest-house or a tacky hostel!

Out of the more than 100,000 or so species of flies in the world, one species has really fallen in love with us and our ways and goes wherever we go! It's a hugely one-sided love affair—we alas don't return their affection nearly as much but try to wham! swat them: not very successfully usually. The common housefly loves us simply because we make muck wherever we go and there's nothing better that they love than something fetid, festering, rotting and stinking to high heavens (especially dung) as the ideal place to bring up their young and feed themselves. A lady housefly can deposit between 350 and 900 eggs (which look like grains of rice) in her lifetime, so obviously population control is not on her mind. And as there's no way we are going to stop making and spreading garbage and sewage, the future of flies is very secure! Their larvae, called maggots, actually clean up a lot of our muck and believe it or not, the maggots of one species—the blow fly—have even found their way inside hospitals where they're used to clean up the charred and dead tissues surrounding horrific burn injuries or around amputation sites. It was accidentally discovered that they were doing this even on battlefields where wounded soldiers lay unattended. (Apparently they do a very neat job, getting rid of the dead tissue without harming any healthy tissue, and secrete anti-bacterial substances on the wound too, thus assisting healing.) And believe it or not, blow-fly larvae are called gentiles! We of course have expressed our gratitude by commercially breeding blow fly and blue-bottle larvae for use as fish-bait and food for carnivorous animals. We've also toyed with the idea of using fly larvae as feed for chickens and pigs, which we farm and eat, though it seems this bright idea has not got many takers.

Maggots have been found useful in another more grisly department too: in murder investigations, or in trying to establish the time of death of a person. Forensic investigators can figure out for how long a person has been dead by checking out the species of maggots to be found crawling over the corpse! Apparently, each species of maggot has a preferred 'best time to eat' and turns up then as if it has booked a table at a fine dining restaurant!

Of course, when you see heaving masses of greasy, cream-looking maggots on a carcass, you're likely to be sick. Adult flies too hum over rotting carcasses and foodstuff and maybe even drop down on that chocolate pastry you were about to take a bite out of even as you try to wave them off. Houseflies can only enjoy a liquid diet and their mouths are specially designed to suck and slurp up stuff. Often, to help their digestive systems, they first vomit all over what they're about to eat, especially if it's semi-solid stuff (I told you they're likely to make you sick), applying digestive enzymes on the food, like a sauce they then sponge up. You might have also noticed that they seem to be very fastidiously cleaning their legs while moving along what they're eating—like someone sanitizing their hands. This is because they taste with their legs and by cleaning their legs, they 'freshen' their taste buds so to speak, just as a wine taster has to 'cleanse his palate' before moving from one wine to another.

Apart from irritating the heck out of us, the flies' disgusting dining habits (the vomiting) also spread a host of very unpleasant diseases. Some of the nastier 'biting' and blood-sucking flies, like the tsetse fly of Africa, which is armed with a stiletto to stab its victims with, spreads sleeping sickness (which affects the brain) and has caused thousands of deaths. River-blindness, another ghastly disease, is spread by black-flies and affects over 20 million people. Black-flies occur in fast-moving streams, their larvae sticking to rocks with suckers and filter feeding with the help of brushes in their mouths. The adults rise in great clouds over humans and animals, and feed by sucking blood, while spreading disease. (All biting flies inject an anti-coagulant into their victims to enable the blood to flow.) Ironically, game wardens and foresters call the tsetse fly the guardian of the forests because people don't venture into the vast territories where they are found, thus protecting the other animals from us.

All in all, flies may spread between thirty and hundred (the figures vary) major diseases amongst us, including elephantiasis, yellow fever, cholera, typhoid, bacillary dysentery and tuberculosis, and can be a special problem in hospitals. During World War II, the Japanese covered houseflies with cholera germs and 'bombed' Chinese cities with them killing 200,000 people. We are such a delightful species, aren't we?

Some of the other unpleasant disease-spreading fly specimens include horse-flies, deer-flies, and sand flies.

Another dynamic and robust (but harmless to us) species is the robber fly which has enormous eyes and a bristly body and hunts other flies, which indicates just how superb a flyer it must be! There are some 225 species in India. One flew into my room, some time back, and landed on the carpet: sadly it was at the fag end of its life, because even as I lay down and photographed it, it keeled over and died. In the garden, on plants, you might have also encountered the metallic iridescent, blue-green long-legged fly, which looks like it's on stilts.

The crane fly or daddy-long-legs belongs to one of the largest fly families, with some 13,500 species, of which more than 1,500 are to be found in India. They're slender, perched on immensely long, spindly legs and like hiding out in foliage that grows in damp humid places. Some may be attracted to and fly towards bright lights.

Basically, flies can be found living virtually in every environment, though most species (excepting the charming housefly) stick to their preferred neck of the woods. But these can include hot springs, septic tanks, sulfur pools and even pools of crude oil. It's thought flies first evolved some 240 million years ago, even before flowering plants, subsisting on honeydew. They can survive in temperatures between -10 and 45 degrees Celsius and as adults have an average lifespan of around a month.

One reason why flies have been so successful globally is because they're strong fliers. They're equipped with just one pair of strong, pliable wings—the forewings. Their hindwings have turned into gyroscopes, flight stabilizers which are called halteres and which help them balance and orient themselves in flight. Flies have two sets of flight muscles, one which gives them the power and the other which manages fine steering control. The halteres vibrate in synchrony with the wing beats and send messages to the steering muscles. (A fly would be unable to fly without its halteres.) The wings can beat independently enabling the fly to change direction in the blink of an eye. They usually fly in a straight line, but if they perceive an obstruction, they can change direction by 90 degrees and continue flying, an action completed in 50 milliseconds! They may be relatively slow on the wing (the horsefly is the fastest clocking 50 kmph). To land on a ceiling, houseflies will approach it dead-on then just before touchdown do a half-roll, pointing all six legs at the ceiling, and making their front legs absorb the shock of the landing before setting down the other four. Their leg ends have a pair of claws with sticky pads in between, which enables them to grip and adhere to the surface. Thus houseflies spread far and wide, reproducing in large numbers. They've also become immune to many of our insecticides and appear to be doing very well in the chemical arms race with us, evolving swiftly to neutralize new insecticides.

Another survival weapon flies (especially houseflies) are equipped with is the way they see. Everyone knows how difficult it is to swat a fly, or grab one in your palm: it's up and away long before the swatter comes down. That's literally because they see in slow motion, slowing action down by seven times, so that they have plenty of time to take evasive action. Can you imagine the plight of pace bowlers if batsmen had this ability! (Batsmen might just fall asleep waiting for the ball.)

Many species of flies are vegans, sucking plant juices, tissue and sap, and are very harmful to agriculture.

There are of course a large number of fly species that are invaluable to us in scientific research (fruit-flies) and pollination (coming second only to bees). Around 6000 species are harmless and often brightly coloured. One of my personal favourites is the hoverfly, simply because of the stunning way in which it flies. Many are striped in yellow and black and look like small bees. They can stand stock-still in mid-air, dodge deftly in any direction they want, even backwards, and are astonishing to watch. None of our aircraft can come even close! It's usually only the males that hover over flowers, seeking the ladies. They live on nectar.

Gentlemen flies of several species such as bee flies and hoverflies and fruit flies guard territories and will drive away interlopers of their own and other species.

Larvae are usually boring creatures with gross appetites and they disgust us, but there's the larva of at least one species of fly—the lacewing or doodle-bug—which is truly diabolical. While the adult is a delicate-looking thing with poor flying capability, the larva is a monster, called the ant-lion. It has a burly body, slender neck and a flattened head crowned with a pair of enormous diabolical sickle-like jaws with hollow barbs, with which it injects venom and digestive juices into its poor victim (usually an ant). It has a bristly body with the bristles aligned such they help it get a firm grip on their victims. Ant-lion larvae don't poop but astonishingly, convert their waste into silk! (Now if only we could also do that!)

They like dry sandy places which are suitable for building their traps. They'll excavate a pit about two inches deep and three inches wide, its sides just steep enough to hold the soil in place but covered in fine loose grains of sands. Other coarser particles are ejected while the digging happens with a toss of the head. The larva, which is very sensitive to motion, then wriggles down backwards to the bottom of the pit and waits. An ant trundles along and finds itself at the rim of the pit. Some of the fine grains of sand give way under its feet and it starts to lose its foothold. As it struggles to regain composure, more grains of sand give way, cascading down the sides of the pit in a mini-avalanche and taking the ant along with it. In a complete panic it flails around desperately, trying to find a foothold and climb back up.

Waiting concealed at the bottom, the ant-lion opens up with a machine-gun like fusillade of sand grains completely upsetting the ant and sending it tumbling down…straight into those monstrous jaws awaiting it at the bottom. They snap up their victim. Then the ant-lion sucks dry its victim and then with a contemptuous toss of the head tosses the husk of the body outside. After this re-sets its trap and awaits its next victim. All so it can turn into a delicate, ballet dancer-like lacewing!

Of course, it's not all hunky-dory for flies. They're hunted down by birds, insects, amphibians, mammals (anteaters) and reptiles as well as falling prey to parasites and fungi. I remember once, at the Sultanpur National Park in Haryana, we came across the carcass of a nilgai, which had probably been brought down by stray dogs. What caught our eye was a heaving mass of bulky green creatures hopping in and out of the stinking bloody carcass. Of course, there were clouds of flies humming en masse all over it. When we checked we discovered that the carcass was crawling and hopping with giant bullfrogs snapping up the flies, as well as maybe snacking on the carcass itself. Well, I thought, all it needed was a gathering or herons and egrets feasting on the frogs to complete the circle of life, but the frogs here looked like total goondas not to be trifled with.

But it's amazing how quickly flies are drawn to a carcass, no matter how big or small. Or for that matter to your mug of beer into which they plunge with all the enthusiasm of an Olympic diver!

There can be nothing more annoying than a mosquito wailing in your ear as you are about to fall asleep. Unfortunately, it can not only be annoying but dangerous too: life-threateningly dangerous. Just three of the around 3500 species of mosquitoes (which belong to the larger clan of flies) in the world are lethal to us and they belong to the notorious families Culex, Anopheles and Aedes. Amongst them, they are responsible for spreading dengue, malaria, chikungunya, yellow fever, Zika, West Nile disease, filariasis and other nasty viruses. Annually they infect some 200 million people killing at least 7 million of them according to one estimate. The WHO estimates an annual death count of 650,000 people due to malaria. Most of the mosquitoes' victims are children and the elderly. As killers they're really in the giant league: according to one account, mosquitoes have been responsible for the deaths of 52 billion people, or half of the total population of the world till now. And believe it or not, the gentlemen mosquitoes are completely innocent in causing all this carnage: it's the ladies that are the wailers and biters, sucking up blood (and infecting their victims in the process) for the iron and proteins, which is necessary for their eggs. The gentlemen are vegans, subsisting on nectar, honeydew and plant juices, which is also what the ladies subsist on when they're not doing their Dracula act.

And get this: we human beings are responsible for passing on the half-baked malaria pathogen to mosquitoes in the first place, which they then processed in their gut to its lethal stage and winged all over the world, spreading the finished product.

Certainly, mosquitoes have shaped human history like no other creature has done. When rapacious white colonizers first sailed to the Americas, they took malaria and yellow fever (and infected mosquitoes) with them on their ships. The local mosquitoes on the continent didn't carry the pathogen, and so the local human population had never encountered malaria. Then, the white man arrived with his dose of the disease passing it on to the local mosquitoes which gave it to the local human population. It's thought that 95 million out of 100 million of the native population died of mosquito-borne diseases (as well as smallpox and influenza), sadly emptying the vast continent so that the white man could gleefully run rampant all over it and claim it all.

That was not all. Malaria and yellow fever killed not only the locals but also the European colonizers and the labour they brought with them on their ships. Then it was discovered that native Africans had developed immunity to malaria on account of having lived with ferocious strains of the disease for centuries in Africa. And so the notorious slave trade began, with slaves that had proven immunity against malaria fetching higher prices than European labour. Malaria, in fact, was partially responsible for the surrender of the British during the American War of Independence having laid low half the British Army at a crucial time.

Mosquitoes have also been used as a weapon of war. Nazis used them during World War II, letting them loose outside Rome. (Much earlier, Florence Nightingale called the Pontine Marshes near Rome 'the valley of the shadow of Death.') Centuries earlier, local, endemic mosquitoes turned back the hordes of Genghis Khan from southern Europe and decimated the forces of Hannibal as he marched through Italy. In one of his skirmishes with the English, Napoleon breached dikes causing brackish floods—lovely breeding grounds for mosquitoes which killed 4000 English soldiers.

As for us, malaria was imported to India (as well as Europe, China and Indonesia) from Africa by European colonizers and local traders, and even today, we are amongst the worst affected nations in the world accounting for 76 per cent of all malaria cases worldwide. In fact, 95 per cent of the country lies in malaria-prone areas.

Of course, mosquitoes don't only have an appetite for human blood. They will go for the blood of any warm-blooded living thing—animals, birds, amphibians and even reptiles. One historian maintains that the dinosaurs (that went extinct 66 million years ago) were already in a decline due to mosquito-borne diseases before the deadly meteorite slammed into the earth. The very earliest and most primitive fossil forms of mosquitoes date back between 90 and 100 million years, while one which more or less resembled our modern mosquitoes went back 79 million years. Mosquitoes have come down virtually unchanged for the last 46 million years, so they seem to have perfected their design!

It's almost impossible to believe that such a tiny, ethereal insect (weighing maybe 0.5 gm) poised en point like a winged ballerina on your arm could wreak such havoc. The posture of the mosquito personally reminds me of the Concorde. Both the insect and the jet have the same predatory downward sloping noses that mean business. So how exactly does Madam Mozzie go about her business (of biting us and sucking our blood)?

Well, for a start, she smells us out. Of the seventy-two odour receptors on her antennae, twenty-seven are tuned to smelling out perspiration. She loves warm, heavy-breathing people who exhale a lot of carbon dioxide and sportspeople who add lactic acid fumes to the mix. She especially loves women who are going to have babies, and people with type O blood. But yes, she has her favourites too—preferring some people over others, those whose body odour appeals to her more. Most mosquitoes operate at dusk and dawn, though there are some (like the dengue-spreading Asian tiger mosquito) that hunt during the day.

She'll spot her victim, circle around it and then land as lightly as a pixie and get to work seeking a soft, suitable spot on the skin. Her mouth parts—the proboscis—are custom-designed for piercing and sucking. The outer sheath, which is visible, bends backwards like a bow as the mosquito begins to bite—it has sense receptors at its tip. Inside hide the cutting and piercing tools which thrust their way into the skin and go deeper, drilling their way in, making the mosquito rock back and forth. A saw-toothed tube catches against the sheath, preventing the stiletto from slipping out when the mosquito moves her head back. Two internal hollow tubes then get to work; one floods the wound with anti-coagulant saliva so that the blood continues to flow, and the other sucks up the blood. It's through these that pathogens may move back and forth between the mosquito and its victim. Once she's tanked up and turgid with blood, she pulls out, leaving an itchy little weal on the skin, which as we all know may turn red. The itchiness is due to our blood's defence systems reacting to the bite. She uses the blood protein she's sucked up purely for the development of her eggs—for herself, she'll subsist on, (like the gentlemen do) on nectar, honeydew and plant juices. But she can take in three times her body weight in blood while she's at it, which makes her easy (and messy) to swat afterwards as she is relatively slow to take off. For the victim there's no significant blood loss though, God knows what pathogens she might have left as a parting present. But often you only realize she's done her deadly work and long gone, when you awake in the morning and contemplate the red bumps on your skin.

Some time later, she'll seek out water—running, still, stagnant or even in a puddle or collected in an old tire (depending on her species) and lay her eggs, usually between 100 and 200. Her larvae, which we must all have seen at some point (those squirming tube-like things with fuzzy mouths), have brush-like mouth parts and wriggle about frantically as they filter out algae and bacteria. They're actually known as wrigglers or wigglers! Both larvae and pupae will dive for cover if threatened. It takes between five and forty days for the eggs to develop into the adult, and while gentlemen live for just about a week (and must mate during this time), the ladies may live up to two weeks in the wild. The gents have bushy antennae made up of auditory sensors with which they tune into the high-pitched hum of the females' wings and recognize her as friend or stranger by her siren song!

So, how can we be rid of mosquitoes and are they of any use at all? Well, getting rid of them could be a problem, since there are estimated to be 100 trillion of them humming around the world at any given time. Also, they are evolving faster than we are quickly becoming immune to every toxic chemical mix we spray on them. We tried DDT and see where that got us! Toxic insecticides kill indiscriminately—the good, the bad and the ugly. Herbal and natural remedies like neem could be used, though it's anyone's guess how long they'll remain effective. To avoid being bitten, we (especially in the developing world) have all slept under mosquito netting and lathered ourselves with mosquito repellent creams. One effective way to discourage them is to get rid of all their possible breeding areas—containers with standing or stagnant water. Also, removing green plants from the house, especially in the evening may be a good idea because that's where they feed and rest.

While malaria still takes a heavy human toll every year, drugs have been developed to counter it. One of the earliest to be discovered was quinine derived from the bark of the chinchona (quina-quina) tree growing in Central and South America, the Caribbean islands and parts of West Africa. While it was extensively used till the 1920s, now synthetic replacements have taken its place. Quinine, like most good drugs, is extremely bitter so to make it more palatable, British soldiers in India added sugar, lime and soda to the concoction. To which, they also added a splash of gin to make the famous gin-and-tonic (G&T), one of the most refreshing alcoholic summer drinks!

Genetic engineers are hard at work trying to manipulate the genes of male mosquitoes so that either they produce offspring which are stillborn or infertile, which would in time render the species extinct; or, to make it impossible for the mosquitoes to pass on the disease pathogens which would get rid of the diseases but not the mosquitoes.

So are mosquitoes complete good-for-nothings? Well, not quite! For one, they are food for myriads of birds, animals, reptiles, amphibians and fish. Secondly, they may actually protect valuable ecosystems that would otherwise be ruined by us. People are loathe to enter vast swamps and marshes because they harbour huge swarms of mosquitoes and these areas (like the Sunderbans) serve as vital habitats for thousands of species of animals, birds, amphibians, reptiles, insects and aquatic life, besides holding and storing water. In the days before it was discovered that malaria was caused by a pathogen, it was thought that the 'bad air' over the marshes caused the disease. ('Mal-air' from which, we got malaria.)

In a similar way (and like the tsetse fly has done) mosquitoes guarded tropical rainforests, keeping us out of them for fear of the disease. So many animals, like rare gorillas, owe them a vote of thanks!

Scientists are also investigating the anti-coagulant property of a mosquito's saliva in the hope of developing blood-thinning drugs and to prevent blood clotting.

Unless you live in Antarctica or Iceland, there's really no getting away from mosquitoes. They're going to keep ruining our evening barbeque parties and gleefully wail about malaria and dengue in our ears just before we drop off to sleep. And while you may feel a sense of satisfaction every time you successfully swat one after it bites you, that uneasy question will continue to lurk at the back of your mind...

Who had this lady bitten before she stabbed you and was she carrying any of those lethal pathogen loads? And what was her 'good' name: Culex Anopheles or Aedes? She never told you.

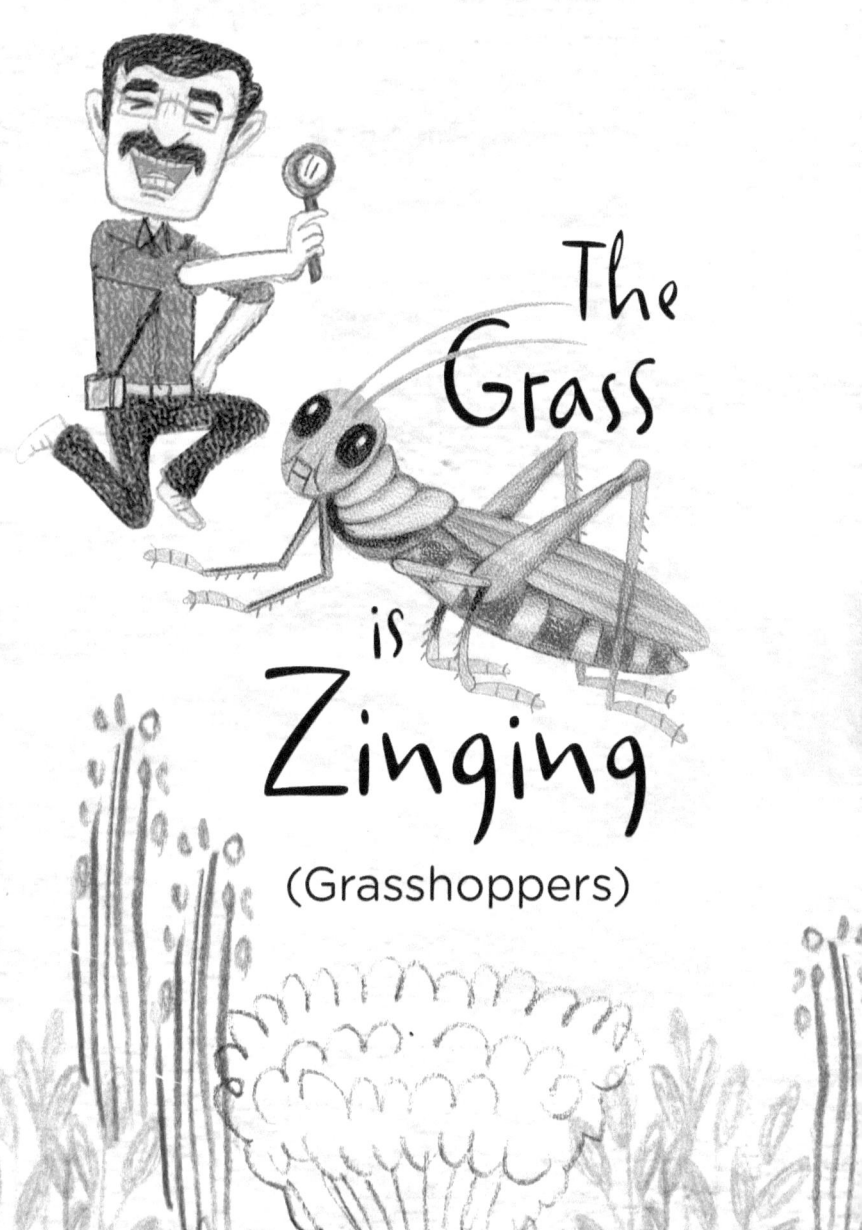

How many times have you tickled a grasshopper? Do it once and you'll immediately want to do it again... and again...until it becomes an addiction: like an itch you just have to tickle, I mean scratch! And it doesn't matter if you are a child or adult: even now I can barely suppress the tendency to gently nudge a grasshopper on its bottom when I see one, just to watch it zing away in one mighty leap. It really is a wonderful way of spending time on the long leg boundary when you are getting bored waiting for the ball to come to you! You can be sure you'll find one in a field if you look carefully enough (they wear camouflage greens and browns) because they're something like over 20,000 species of them in the world and they prefer the tropics. They've been roughly divided into two camps: the short-horned grasshoppers (estimates vary up to 12,000 species of these), and long-horned grasshoppers and crickets, which the Americans like to call katydids.

It's the short-horned variety that comprise the prodigious leapers. If we could jump as far, we'd be able to cross the length of a football field in a single leap. It's astonishing considering that grasshoppers can leap ten times their own height! All this without a wing unfurling! Now how cool is that!

The long-horned grasshoppers (usually clad in green or brown) can't match this and their cousins, the crickets, usually dressed in browns and blacks often creep into our houses at night and chirp away to potential girlfriends. Some long-horned grasshoppers live in aquatic vegetation, and normally they lay a single egg at a time. Actually, all grasshoppers 'sing' or stridulate by rubbing their tooth-edged legs against their wings, somewhat like you drawing a comb across a rough surface. It's generally the gentlemen that 'sing' to woo the ladies and each species has its own special song. In some species, even the ladies join in.

These fairly large insects are well equipped for their role in the world. They have big compound eyes, with near all-round vision, and hearing organs (called tympani) located in their abdomens. Their bodies and sensitive antennae are covered with fine hairs which pick up scent and the faintest stirring of a breeze. And who can forget those massive thunder thighs which catapult them away from danger. Many have wings and can fly well. They also have prodigious appetites and in locust avatar can eat their own weight in vegetation every day. Most are vegans, though some, especially of the long-horned clan also go in for delicious animal juices and succulent feces. Needless to add, the vegans are not looked upon favourably by most farmers, gardeners and horticulturalists.

Normally, a grasshopper is a happy-go-lucky solitary individual, but at least twenty species have a deadly (for us) avatar when they turn into locusts. Here in India, we have three varieties: the Bombay locust, the desert locust, and the migratory locust. So how exactly does this Dr Jekyll and Mr Hyde change take place? When conditions are good and plenty of green stuff is available, and the rains have been bountiful, grasshoppers, especially those living in arid areas and near deserts have a tendency to cluster together. Once a critical number is reached and each potential desert locust has a certain number of 'friends', their little brains begin to release serotonin—the magic chemical that makes you and me and all living creatures very happy. In the grasshoppers' case this means that they become very hungry indeed and they fall headlong in love with each other and produce babies—called 'nymphs'—en masse. Eggs, between 100 and 200, are laid in the soft earth in 'pods' and hatch into tiny wingless replicas of their parents. From drab brown camouflage colours (remember, these guys usually live in arid, tan coloured areas), the erstwhile grasshoppers change into bright yellow and black to warn predators that they are poisonous; not that this is entirely necessary since by now their numbers explode into the millions, so the chances of any single one being picked out are remote. And now they begin to eat everything in sight, demolishing crops at a scale that can cause famines in countries. On the ground, billions of their babies, now known as 'hoppers', clean up from the ground up while their parents feed higher up, and when done, take to the air in gigantic swarms to seek new pastures. When the 'front line' lands to feed, those bringing up the rear fly over them and ahead and so the swarm advances.

Their numbers can be staggering. A single swarm can cover an area of 26 square kilometers and weigh 300 tons (which is also the amount of food they consume each day) and this number can go up to 780 square kilometers! The largest locust swarm recorded was of the Rocky Mountain locust (ironically now extinct) which was 2900 km long (more than the distance from Delhi to Mumbai and back by air!) and 180 km wide and contained an estimated 3.5 trillion insects.

Large swarms can have billions of locusts, as many as 80 million per square kilometer. It's no surprise therefore that locust swarms are the farmers' worst nightmare, sweeping across the country devouring every green plant they come across. In India, our desert locust is one of the chief culprits and normally hangs around on the borders of the Thar Desert and in Rajasthan. Africa has huge conglomerations too, which are not averse to migrating east and causing problems in India.

As these insects have been around for close to 250 million years, they have caused famines throughout human history. They are mentioned in the Bible, the Koran and the Mahabharata. They plagued ancient Egyptian and Greek civilizations too.

To be sure, they have their own enemies and try to evade being hunted by wearing either camouflage colours, or by suddenly flashing startlingly bright colours on their unfurling wings to scare hunters away. But blister beetles, spiders, wasps and robber flies eat their 'nymphs', while birds and mammals enjoy the adults. It's said that the rosy-starling times its breeding season with the advent of locusts so that their babies would have plenty of high-protein fare. The highly endangered great Indian bustard also enjoys gobbling up locusts after chasing them around. Other animals, like jackals, wildcats and rodents also enjoy locusts. As for us, we fry and grill and smoke them crispy and crunch them up in China, Japan, Indonesia, Africa, the

Middle East and Mexico. We have to be careful that they're not laced with insecticides though!

They are plagued by their own pathogens and parasites and fungi too and we have attempted to eradicate them (locusts especially) using insecticides or by bio-control methods such as using a killer fungus that only targets them. We're now (in killjoy manner) trying to develop an insecticide which will suppress the production of serotonin in them so that they don't go into locust mode and turn them into zombies instead. We also use eagle-eyed surveillance to nip swarms in the bud before they go out of control. In India, we've also tried using drones to spray them apart.

Grasshoppers can have their uses too. They help in maintaining a balance in the variety of plants that grow by making sure none really exceeds its brief and becomes a problem. When they die a normal death, microbes process their bodies and release stored nitrogen into the soil, which again is useful for the growth of carbohydrate rich plants. But when they're in a state of fear and stress, they tend to eat more carbohydrates, which microbes find difficult to process and release, now enabling nitrogen rich plants to thrive. And believe it or not, for plants, grasshopper droppings are more nutritious than cowpat manure!

In these troubled times, scientists and researchers have recently discovered that grasshoppers can be used as bomb or explosive detectors! Robo-grasshoppers were strapped on with featherweight backpack sensors, which picked up electrical signals from the insects' antennae and fed these signals into a computer. Somehow the grasshoppers were able to detect the presence of high concentrations of explosives and this message was conveyed back to a computer. A team of seven grasshoppers pinpointed the presence of explosives accurately 80 per cent of the time, while a single individual was successful just 60 per cent of the time.

But, as mentioned earlier, grasshoppers have thrilled both children and adults (and especially adults who are children) by the manner in which they zing off when tickled on their bottoms. Just how do they do it? To put it simply, they work like catapults, storing up large quantities of energy and releasing them in an instant. The massive rear leg of the grasshopper consists of three sections: the thigh, the shin and the foot. Inside the thigh are two separate muscles—one running along the underside of the thigh called the 'flexor' muscle, and another, far more powerful one, called the 'extensor' muscle. Both are connected to the thigh bone by tendons. At the point where the thigh meets the shin is a mass of tough, elastic cuticle, a little lump of tough protective material, which is also attached to the massive extensor muscle. Before leaping, the grasshopper focuses on the job at hand and suspends all other activities like eating or singing.

Inside the thigh, the flexor muscle now begins to contract, drawing up the shin into the correct position for blast-off. The foot is pressed down flat and hard against the take-off surface, which could be a leaf or the ground. The grasshopper is now like a sprinter on the blocks. Now the all-powerful extensor muscle begins to contract, slowly but powerfully, like when you pull back on a bow or pull a catapult's rubber. The elastic cuticle bulges as it stores the energy just the way a bow bends when you pull back on an arrow. It has stored all the energy drawn up by the extensor muscle for the leap. Then the flexor muscle suddenly relaxes and boing! all the energy is released in a burst by the cuticle, enabling the grasshopper to catapult away to safety. The forces generated by the leap could be twenty times the force of gravity (20g). It's said that grasshoppers that are spooked into jumping go much farther than when jumping voluntarily—which is no surprise really. The grasshopper may even use this powerful kick as a mode of self-defence— what a karate kick it would be— and even spits when feeling threatened. But frankly, I would think it's worth risking getting kicked and spat on, just to see these big-eyed insects zing away when you gently tickle their bums!

Spyder, Spyder, Hairy Fright

(Spiders)

Spiders gross most people out. Some scream and faint with fright when they see one, others pick up the nearest rolled up newspaper or magazine and WHAM! And often the big brooms come out to sweep them and their cobwebs out. This is strange really, because they avidly take down flies, mosquitoes and cockroaches.

Personally, I love spiders. Oh no, this doesn't mean I keep cuddly 'teddy bear' tarantulas in my shirt pocket but I will happily share a bathroom with them if necessary and watch them set their traps or pounce lightning fast on pests. And even the most avid spider-hater will be gobsmacked if they observe an orb-web pearled with dew or raindrops, like ropes of necklaces hanging between twigs.

We still seem uncertain about how many species of spiders exist—estimates range from 48,200 to 90,000; one of the smallest being the Samoan moss spider, just 0.011 of an inch long, and the largest, the fearsome Amazonian Goliath bird–eating spider, with a foot span of 12 inches, enough to cover your face! They are hugely useful to us: collectively the world's 25 million tons of spiders consume between 400 and 800 million tons of crop-destroying pests, so we ought to doff our hats to them every time we see them. Spiders in their present form evolved between 318 and 299 million years ago; because they're soft-bodied they do not form fossils well (except if trapped in amber), so it is tough to come by accurate records. They're found worldwide except as usual, in Antarctica.

All spiders are locked and loaded with venom though very few are dangerous to us—the black widow and the brown recluse being the most notorious of these and both are good citizens of the United States. It's another story for the spiders' victims, who are first stabbed by the fearsome down-curved fangs, and paralyzed by the venom pumped in and then slowly liquefied by the digestive juices the spider injects. The liquid 'soup' is then sucked back in (spiders don't do solid foods). Some victims may just be enshrouded in silk and kept for another time if the spider isn't that hungry.

The other big USP of spiders is their ability to spin silk. Now other insects, such as caterpillars, do produce silk as well but none make so much use of it as spiders. Silk, a protein, is produced in the silk glands and squeezed out in fluid form (like toothpaste) from taps or spigots on the spider's abdomen from its spinnerets. The orb weaver's lower abdomen is crammed with 600 silk glands of different varieties, each of which has a specialized function. The fluid silk solidifies into strands, not on contact with air, but when the spider pulls it taut, as this changes the molecular structure of the protein. It's a pretty specialized product because there are six or seven varieties of silk that are produced, depending on their use. Thus, the silk used to cocoon eggs is different from the silk used for web construction and here too there are qualitative differences: silk used for web-scaffolding is different to the silk strands which are covered with glue to trap victims. Web-silk is stronger and more elastic than steel wire of the same thickness and is similar to other super tough natural substances such as chitin, cellulose and collagen. I read somewhere that if a spider was to spin a huge web, with silk strands as thick as a pencil, it would be able to stop a Boeing 747 in mid-flight! If you've ever walked into a web in a forest, you may have been surprised at the sheer tenacity of the silk thread that often feels like glass-coated kite string.

Not all spiders spin webs as traps. In fact, the majority don't. Hunting and jumping spiders ambush their prey using sheer speed or camouflage, but they will unravel a silk safety line behind them every time they jump. Web weavers, too, adopt different types of webs. A few 'social' spiders will build huge communal tent webs with multiple entrances, others build the higgledy-piggledy cobwebs in the corners of houses which moms so hate. The most renowned certainly are the orb-weavers, whose dew-drenched webs remind us of pearl necklaces.

So how are these marvels of civil engineering constructed? We've been so impressed we're seeing if their design can be used for sports stadiums and other large constructions. Some wily spiders build their own modest edifices at the edge of a magnificent orb-web and dart in and steal the prey that gets trapped in it, before the web-builder knows what's happening.

All the amazing web-building hardware is hardwired into the spider's little brain. But it is clever enough to adapt to the location when necessary. Two broad building principles are followed. First, the outer framework of the web is constructed—like the frame of a picture. Then the radial lines are laid, symmetrically so that the web's balance is not upset, spanning out from the centre of the web. Finally, the spirals are unraveled—twice over, the first time with non-sticky silk so the spider can move around without getting stuck herself, and the second time with the gluey silk. The exact technique used by spiders may differ.

Web building is a complex process with different methods being used by different species. Basically, the spider must first be able to anchor a line across two objects, say twigs or branches, by loosening out a strand of silk into the wind, and hoping it will catch. Once this happens, she begins constructing the framework of the web. This may have four sides (as in a picture frame) or be Y-shaped. To-ing and fro-ing from the centre, she now affixes radial lines from here to the framework of the web until she has twenty or more radiating from the hub. All this has been done using non-sticky silk. Back from the centre, she now spirals anti-clockwise towards the edge of the web, affixing non-sticky silk to the radial lines. At the edge, she reverses direction and spirals back towards the centre, extruding sticky silk as she goes (stretching and twanging the line as she affixes them to the radial line so that beads of glue adhere evenly) and consuming the silk she had laid down earlier. From the centre she may or may not construct a zigzag X-shaped pattern called decorations or stabilmenta, which some believe serve as warning to birds who may otherwise crash into and destroy the web. Web building usually happens in the evenings or very early morning. Some orb weavers construct horizontal webs to catch insects flying up or down into them.

Once done the spider crouches either in the hub of her web, or if she's a 'fraidy cat, at one corner and awaits her meal. It's not long coming as butterflies (I once saw eleven get trapped one after another—the poor spider was beside herself!), dragonflies, flies and grasshoppers fly into them. They struggle—apparently as many as 50 per cent may escape. Once they tire out comes the spider! One bite paralyzes them. If she's hungry, she'll suck up their life juices then and there, if not, she'll shroud them in silk and keep them for when she is hungry.

Most spiders however, actively hunt down their prey, some using silk, others not. The ogre-faced spider holds a net of silk between her widespread front claws and waits in ambush for an insect to arrive beneath her. When one is in range, she flings the net lightning fast over her victim.

The bolas spider extrudes a strand of silk at the end of which is a sticky ball of silk. She waits for gentlemen moths, alluring them with the perfume of lady-moths and when they flutter close, she swings the sticky ball at them, thus trapping them.

Trapdoor spiders, which are nocturnal, build funnel webs in the ground, some covered with a silken trapdoor and with trip-lines set just outside. An insect stumbles on these, its vibrations are picked up and the spider is out and on it in a trice. The diving bell spider builds a silken dome just under water, buoying it up with bubbles of air trapped (and then rubbed) in her hairy body so she can breathe. She waits for an aquatic insect or tadpole to snag against the web—and lunch is served.

Wolf and crab spiders wait in ambush. The latter may hide in flowers and are often the exact shade of the petals—white, pink or yellow. I once met a pearl white one on a madhumalti creeper, virtually invisible, holding a massive bee in her jaws.

I love watching the highly strung jumping spiders on the walls, unlike most spiders, they have excellent vision—telephoto and binocular—and their eyes are really quite beautiful, poised like the headlamps of cars on their heads. They may see ten times better than dragonflies, which have the best sight in the insect world. The jumpers posture and feint like boxers in a ring following your every move… If you are a fly and within range they leap so fast you can't quite see them go, but they do trail a safety silken line behind them. In fact, there's one species of jumping spider, belonging to the Portia clan, which actually displays intelligence while planning an attack. She's a spider-eating spider so has to be especially careful, deviously planning her attack from her victim's blind side.

Sometimes I think we don't give spiders enough credit. A spider once built her small web in the corner of my bathroom, virtually at floor level. I thought she was nuts—nothing really would come her way. But she'd figured it out. Her trap was smack in the pathway used by big black ants perambulating about from one side of the bathroom to the other. She caught at least one every day for over a week!

In the undergrowth the furry tarantulas prowl, searching for small creatures. The massive bird-eating Goliath spider will happily dine off mice, frogs, squirrels and even small birds. Except for one species of jumping spider, the intriguingly named, *Bagheera kiplingi* found in South America, all spiders are hardcore carnivores. But the vegan Bagheera feeds on pollen and nectar for the most (90 per cent) of her diet.

If you are a gentleman spider, your love life is fraught with danger. Often, you will be several times smaller than your lady love, twenty times smaller and thousand times lighter (except if you're a jumping spider) and she usually has food more on her mind than fun. You will spend your time wandering around, looking for her and when you find her, you must be careful. Very careful: Sitting in the middle of her kingdom, she is formidable, ferocious, shortsighted, short-tempered, and usually hungry. Depending on your species, you might think it proper to take her a gift—a silk-wrapped cockroach will do nicely or play her some harp music by twanging the strands of her web that lull her into a state of yogic calmness. If you have a gift, you will offer it, and while she's excitedly unraveling it, do your bit—and beat it! You can only hope that your harp music will bemuse her enough to let you do your duty and you might even dare to tie her up with silk to ensure she can't suddenly pounce on you. In many cases, however, you will turn out to be the dinner and the date but as you are being liquefied, just think that really you (and she) are doing this for your kids! The protein she sucks up from you will do her eggs a world of good making the babies strong and healthy. There is one species in which the gallant gentleman has his honeymoon, escapes, and then deliberately returns in order to be eaten. Now how noble is that!

The jumping spiders have a less ferocious love life. The gorgeous dancing peacock spider—all multi-hued—will do a wonderful dance routine while courting his lady. In many species, the gents are more glamorous than their ladies. Tarantulas also dance, but here the gentleman's intention is usually to hold the lady at a 'safe distance', so she doesn't get close enough to sink her fangs into him!

Spider moms can be both great and bizarre. Eggs are usually carefully laid on a silken mat, as many as 3000 of them, rolled up in an egg case. This the spider mom guards like a Rottweiler. A glassy-looking lynx spider once furiously emerged from her leaf hideout to deal with my probing twig, and when it rained, she dragged her egg case under the cover of leaves. When the baby spiderlings hatch, they may actually beg to be fed, and the mom obliges by bringing them her kills or regurgitating them. At least in one species, the supreme sacrifice is made: the spider mom offers herself up as a meal for her myriad babies—which they indulge in with gluttonous gusto. Actually, when food is scarce, the spiderlings may turn on one another and if mom is hungry too, she may also snack off some of her babies. I've watched sibling rivalry at work: angel-white lynx spiderlings busily trying to knock one another off a strand of the web rather like what happened when Robin Hood first met Little John across the stream. When spiderlings are old enough to leave home, they climb up to a convenient stalk, stick their bums into the air, heads down, extrude a strand of silk which catches the breeze and bears them aloft. Some have even been found clinging to airplane windows! But they can decide when and where they want to land.

They simply roll up the strand of silk into a ball and get back on to the ground.

Spiders have many enemies: birds, wasps, lizards—and humans—who will eat them. Wasps famously paralyze spiders with their sting and cache them away, laying an egg on them, which hatches into a grub that eats the spider from the inside out, keeping the vital organs for last. The wasp mom has ensured her grub gets fresh meat—and plenty of it!

Spiders have derived numerous ways to escape. Many are cryptically coloured to match their surroundings, others turn out in gaudy shades to show they're poisonous. Some play dead, some run like hell, zigzag even, and others mimic inedible insects. Webs too may be vibrated to confuse enemies, giving the spider enough time to run for it. The golden wheeling spider of the Namibian desert curls itself into a ball and rolls down the dunes at top speed like tumbleweed in the wind! Some hairy spiders flick the hair off their bodies with their legs at their enemies. The hair greatly irritates the skin of the enemy and is like a nettle, but is not venomous. Normally spiders live for about two years, though some tarantulas have lived for over twenty-five years in captivity.

Apart from eating spiders, we destroy their habitat despite them being among the best pest controllers. In fact, we're researching the use of spider venom for bio-friendly pesticide as well as in medicine for treating heart issues, Alzheimer's and strokes.

We're trying to spin spider silk in large quantities by using their genes in goats to see if we can produce silk from their milk! There can be many uses for spider silk; from gun-sights to surgical sutures, and making of light bulletproof jackets and seat belts in cars! Researchers have extracted a strand of silk more than 100 metres long from a single spider. Minute air pollutants also get stuck on the strands of sticky silk and we can analyse them to know what pollutants are in the air.

Many humans suffer from arachnophobia which is an irrational fear of spiders and everything linked with them: Probably because the creatures are hairy and prowl about in dark corners giving them the frights. But really many of them are just stunning in appearance and feisty in character. So much so that I've rewritten William Blake's famous lines in his poem, 'The Tyger': I call it 'The Spyder' of course!

The Spyder

Spyder, spyder hairy fright,
In the cobwebs of the night
What immortal hand or eye
Hath carved thy silken symmetry?

The Sting is in the (Scorpions) Tail

I have to admit that I've never been able to get as close and personal with scorpions as I would have liked to, chiefly because they're so hard to see, especially during the day. The last time I encountered one was on the Northern Ridge in Delhi years and years ago and it scuttled off as fast as it could. They really are creatures, or should we say, arachnids of the night and have a strong aversion to light. (It's called being photophobic.) But these ancient—over 435 million year old—armoured creatures can capture your imagination like few of its relatives (mites and ticks ugh!) can. They always remind me of medieval gladiators, entering an arena with their maces raised high as they maneuver and joust for positions from which they can plunge that deadly hooked barb (called the telson) into their adversary's body. Back in their time (435 million years ago) some could grow to 3 feet in length—imagine one of those coming after you—and migrated from the oceans on to the land. They may have shrunk in size, the largest is now 18 cm long, the average being 6 cm, but their basic design has been largely unchanged indicating that Nature got it right first time.

Scorpions have crawled and scuttled to nearly every corner of the globe (except Antarctica) and where they were not originally found, like New Zealand, they've reached by hitching rides on our ships and planes. They really do prefer the deserts to other habitats and can tolerate temperatures of up to 47 degrees Celsius (after which they just bury themselves in the sand or stand with their bodies above the surface—like doing a push-up without coming back down). Desert-dwelling scorpions are usually light fawn and brown to match with the sand, while those found lurking under rocks or behind barks and inside crevices in walls are darker brown or black.

What makes a scorpion a scorpion is of course that wickedly barbed stinger it curls high over its back with its bulbous venom glands. All scorpions are armed with venom, though of the 1750 described species (again, the number varies depending on which source you're looking at) only between twenty-five and forty (again estimates vary widely) can be deadly to us. Their venom is pretty specialized, there can be as many as forty-five different toxins in them. Different concoctions are used for different insect prey, more powerful ones for small mammals and reptiles like lizards and snakes. In addition, the scorpion can regulate the amount, potency and exact formulation of the venom it is injecting into its victim, usually enough to paralyze or kill it. Like a doctor's compounder in the old days used to mix the ingredients for a drug, so the scorpion combines the various compounds in its venom so that it may be custom-made for the victim! If the victim is not too big or strong, the scorpion simply crushes it with its massive pincer-like jaws (called pedipalps), chews it up with special pincer-like 'cutlery' outside its mouth while vomiting digestive juices over it, before sucking down the resulting liquid. Like the spider, it lives on a liquid diet. Apart from hunting, the scorpion will use its stinger in defence when it is under attack by its own predators. While scorpion stings may be painful and dangerous, we have anti-venom for all of them so fatalities are rare. (But it's better to get to a hospital.) We are, in fact, researching the use of their venom for treating rheumatoid arthritis, Alzheimer's disease and multiple sclerosis.

Scorpions come into their own at night; during the day they hide under rocks or in crevices and underground burrows. While their eyesight is poor, in spite of having six to eight eyes, they are acutely sensitive to light. So much so that at night they can find their way around and hunt by starlight. One feature, which we still haven't figured, is why exactly their armour-plated exoskeleton absorbs ultraviolet light and reflects it back as an eerie green visible light, a phenomenon called fluorescence. Researchers use ultraviolet light to search for them at night, for the creatures glow in the dark like some ancient medieval monsters!

In spite of not being able to see too well, scorpions are well-equipped to hunt in the dark. The tops of their bodies, or the dorsal section, is covered with very fine hairs that deflect with the slightest disturbance, enabling the scorpion to precisely gauge the distance and direction of a flying insect. Its massive pincers too are covered with sensitive hairs and God help, the insect that accidentally brushes against them! The lower section of its body, the ventral section, is acutely sensitive to vibrations in the ground as well as to alluring perfume (pheromones), emitted by the lady. When boy scorpion meets girl scorpion, he does what boy humans have done with girl humans since forever—he takes her dancing in the dark! He'll hold her massive pincers with his own and execute his steps, backwards and sideways, his kisser of a stinger hovering lovingly over her. Sometimes he might actually kiss her with it too, but not injecting enough venom to hurt or harm her (maybe it just tingles). He'll move around trying to find a nice flat dance floor, and when he succeeds, will deposit a packet of sperm (this is like social distancing gone nuts) on the ground and gently draw her over it so she can squat on it and absorb it into the opening in her body, where it fertilizes her eggs. I really would love to see 'glow-in-the-dark' scorpions waltzing around in a cemetery perhaps to the strains of the 'Blue Danube' waltz being played by a full orchestra! The honeymoon can last anywhere between an hour to more than a day. If all this makes the lady irritably peckish, she might even eat her husband afterwards.

Scorpion babies (scorpionlings) are born two to eighteen months later, emerging one by one, fully formed, white and bulbous. They are soft and helpless and can neither eat nor protect themselves. The average number of births varies between eight and twenty-five, but a litter may have anything between 1 and 200 babies. Until they moult (shed their exoskeleton) the first time, they live on their egg yolk sac and absorb moisture from their mom's body by climbing onto her back and clinging on. Here they may stay between one and fifty days; some scorpion moms spoil their babies rotten, by hunting prey for them. The hulking bachchas naturally hang around mom for as long as two years! However, it may be dangerous; if mom is hungry and ceases to recognize them once they get off her back (after moulting the first time) she may eat them! In the wild, they may live between three and five years if they are not eaten.

They must moult five to seven times before they can have babies of their own.

Most scorpions prefer staying in their burrows and wait for prey to come to them. A few are active hunters, though they may do so for just a few hours. They have a very slow metabolic rate (their energy needs are low and so they burn less fuel) and can survive in extreme conditions, heat or cold. While they can eat upto one-third their own weight in one sitting, they can also go without food for as long as a year and on average, may have between five and fifty meals a year. Chiefly, they hunt insects (and each other) and are useful in keeping insect pest numbers under control. They can live at sea level (one species has been discovered at a depth of 800 metres) or up in the mountains (the Andes and Himalayas) 3000 metres above sea level! They can be super-cooled, having stayed below freezing for weeks and then will return to normal activity within a few hours of thawing and can be immersed in water for one or two days, without any ill effects. Those dwelling in the desert have feet specially adapted so they don't sink into the porous sand, and rock-climbers have rock-climbing boots! Some scorpions even sing, rather in the manner that crickets do, by rubbing their legs together. However, they do not sing love songs but warning anthems—stay away from me, or else!

In spite of their ferocious reputation as creatures not to be trifled with, scorpions have legions of enemies out there to eat them. This includes themselves. Cannibalism can be quite a problem, because it reduces their numbers significantly. They are thought to be so aggressive with each other that they're called 'inveterate cannibals'. But birds, and animals such as meerkats and mongooses also crunch them up, first disarming them by removing their stings. Meerkats and mongooses are immune to scorpion venom.

Scorpions, especially the venomous ones, can cause us a lot of distress and so, when you're in a place where they're likely to be (dry deserts, humid rainforests, etc) it's better to shake out your clothes, sheets, towels, socks and footwear before using them, because they love tucking away in dark nooks and crannies. They're well known for snuggling up right at the toe end of dark, cozy bedroom slippers!

We've often regarded scorpions as the embodiment of evil and danger and aggressiveness. We've named tanks and battleships after them. The ancient Egyptian goddess Isis was linked with scorpions because she was as devoted a mother as scorpions are!

There's one unsolved mystery that still hangs around these antediluvian looking creatures. We still don't know *why* they glow in the dark!

Well, if you carry your house on your back and take it along with you everywhere, you are hardly likely to have the speed of an Olympic sprinter. And so snails, which do this, top out at approximately 1 mm per second or 0.0036 kmph. But some, apart from lugging their houses around, can also pull fifty times their own weight. Also, they have to kind of make their own road, laying down a layer of glutinous mucus, which can be thick or thin depending on the terrain they have to traverse. They can, if needed, lay down such a glutinous coating of mucus that they can glide over the sharp straight edge of a razor blade without cutting themselves. The smallest snail can pass through the eye of a needle, shell and all, while the largest, the gross African land snail can grow to 15 inches and weigh a whopping 1 kg. On average, they live between two and seven years though this can go up to ten years in the larger species and even twenty-five years for those in captivity.

The first snails were thought to roam about on the sea bed some 580 million years ago (they had gills) after which some migrated to the land (they developed lungs) some 286 million years ago. Sea snails, which are more numerous in species and much more glamorous, as well as freshwater snails still trundle along on the ocean floor or river and stream beds. Snails are boneless, soft-bodied mollusks or 'shelled gastropods'. Today, there are about 35,000 species of land snails undulating their way across gardens, undergrowth, trees, bushes and hedges mostly coming out at night. Most are vegans which devour leaves and plant material, and one or two species are predatory carnivores. Many species are regarded as pests, though on the upside, they also provide a valuable food (and calcium) source for small animals, birds and large insects—and us. (The French call them escargots when they cook them in their fancy restaurants.) Of course snails duck back into their shells while being attacked, but this doesn't faze many predators who either break the shell and pull them out or crunch them up shell and all, thus improving their calcium intake.

You know, life gets complicated enough when you develop a crush on someone and are not quite sure that person fancies you in return. But the love life of some snail species goes much beyond just that! You see, in these species, each snail is both boy-snail and girl-snail *at the same time!* And well, when they want to have baby snails—that's when things get properly weird.

First, of course, they have to meet each other. They use their lower pair of tentacles to detect each other's delectable perfumes. The top longer pair of tentacles have a mustard-seed sized pinpoint eye, which doesn't see that well, and snails are deaf. Their lower shorter pair of tentacles feels the ground as they make their way to one another. Once they are convinced that they are of the same species and kind of like one another, they begin courting, coming closer to each other, touching tentacles, and even kissing. They take their time about this from a couple of hours to maybe half the day. What they're actually trying to do is to maneuver themselves into a suitable position, for something truly shocking to follow. Because now it's almost time for them to actually make out! Now boy snail wants to have babies with girl snail. Well, just when you think all is lovey-dovey between them, what do they do? They get up close, almost bumping chests like sportspersons do, and from their necks, pfft! shoot out a harpoon or 'love dart' crafted out of calcium or chitin, the size of a fingernail into each other. (Apparently this is where we got the idea for Cupid's arrow.) Often they're not very careful about their aim and may seriously injure their partners or miss completely, which happens maybe 30 per cent of the time. The shooting of darts and harpoons is of course a very boy thing to do, and it is indeed done at the initiative of the boy half of the snails. Some say that the snails being shot thus, find it pleasurable, some say it's painful and they try to avoid it but who really knows? After shooting each other they come together and make out. But still all is not hunky dory.

What is known is that the dart is covered with mucus loaded with hormones and suchlike chemicals which prevent the killing and digestion of as many sperms as possible belonging to the shooter, when they enter the girl snail. At the same time the hormones put off the girl snail from making out with other boy snails thereafter. When say boy snail shoots his dart, this is what he has in mind for his relationship with girl snail: she should have only his babies.

Girl snail (or for that matter all girl snails) however, would rather make out with as many boy snails as possible to have a variety in her children, which would improve their chances of survival. Her internal plumbing is specially designed to actually kill off or digest as many of the boy snail's wriggling sperm (more than 99 per cent) before they can reach the safety of a special pouch, where they may be stored and used to fertilize eggs. To do this, they have to pass through a very long tunnel and bypass a nasty container where sperm is digested, an obstacle course, rather like the police roadblocks and diversions we find everywhere. The hormonal chemicals in the boy snail's dart prevent the digestion of as many as possible of his sperm, so that they reach the safety of the pouch intact in maximum numbers.

It's thought that the boy snail which gets in his harpoon first, or has the bigger, sharper harpoon, has a better chance to make babies than one who is slower on the draw. The chemicals on his harpoon also narrow and block the tunnel through which any subsequent sperm contributed by some ruffian roadside Romeo snail can make its way, so that it dies, or gets digested. Already snug in the storage pouch, the first shooter's sperm can then fertilize the lady's eggs at leisure.

So it seems that boy snail and girl snail are working at cross purposes: boy snail wants as many babies as possible, on the condition they must be only his (so only his magnificent genes get passed on), and girl snail also wants to have babies, but by different papas so there's a better chance of her babies surviving. (If it was to be only one partner for her and he turned out to have wacko genes, where would that leave her and her babies?)

It's believed that both parties are trying to evolve further to improve their chances: the boy snails by lengthening and sharpening their harpoons (which for us would be like throwing a 15-inch kitchen knife), the girl snails by improving their blocking and digesting mechanisms and maybe even by growing harder skins to deflect the harpoon.

Once they have mated, the mama goes off and digs a shallow pit in which to lay and bury her eggs.

But can you imagine the conversation between a mama snail and her babies, when she tries to explain the facts of life to them just before they set off into the world on their own?

Mama Snail:	*Babies, gather around. I have something to tell you. I'm also a he!*
Babies:	*What? But you're mama—a she!*
Mama:	*Part of me is a he. So you could say I'm a she-he.*
Babies:	*What about papa then?*
Mama:	*Well, part of him is also a she. So he's a he-she.*
Babies:	*What? Then what are we: He-shes or she-hes?*
Mama:	*It doesn't matter, now slime along babies and find a suitable girl and boy for yourselves.*

Luckily for mama snails, they trundle off before their babies hatch and can ask such awkward questions. Of course not all snails are like this, some are only either girl snails or boy snails, while some change from one to another every season.

Baby snails emerge perfectly formed and begin growing their shells around their bodies. Their internal organs are protected by a special layer of tissue called the mantle, and it is this mantle that secretes the calcium that is required for the formation of the shell, which takes place in the familiar spiral shape. Snails must get a good amount of calcium in their diet to develop strong shells. Once the snail is mature, the shell stops growing and thickens around its opening. As snails must always remain moist, or they dehydrate and die, they can seal the opening of their shells with dried mucus and curl up inside if it gets too dry, or for that matter too cold. While hibernating they can drop their pulse from 36 beats per minute to 3 or 4 and their oxygen requirement by one-fiftieth!

Much to their astonishment, scientists discovered that snails are pretty brainy, and have good memories! Apparently, their brains work in much the same way as ours. Only their brains are too tiny and have too few nerve cells and wiring connections between them to enable them to argue with us on TV debates.

We have long relished snails as delicacies. Actually, in ancient times, Roman soldiers carried snails in their pockets as food. Now they are served in fancy restaurants all over Europe and even their eggs are called snail caviar! They can be cooked in many ways, but have to be cooked very thoroughly to get rid of unpleasant parasites. The giant African land snail, among others, often harbours the nasty rat lungworm larvae, which it gets after ingesting rat feces (what a dish to dine on!), and these larvae lodge in our brains after we've eaten infected snails causing a terrible form of meningitis and a very unpleasant death. From their home in East Africa, these giant purplish snails have infiltrated to the far corners of the globe—including India—and with a diet of over 500 species of plants, are regarded as a major pest species. There were hordes of them on the Delhi Ridge several monsoons ago, emerging from behind tree barks when the rains arrived. Their shells are sharp enough to puncture car tires and certainly make a horrible crunching sound when you (accidentally) step on them.

I have to admit, while I'm game to try everything at least once, I would probably draw the line at snails. It really would seem like prising out large globs of snot from the shell and putting them in your mouth. And who the heck likes eating boogers covered in mucus?

A Hundred, Thousand Feet

(Centipedes and Millipedes)

There I was cooling off in the shower when a movement caught my eye. They widened in horror. From the sinkhole, a long, pale grey, very bristly monster emerged, its long feelers waving this way and that… 'Anything to kill? Anything to kill? Anything to kill?'

Then it spotted my bare feet and charged towards them at about 90 kmph. I emitted a yell of alarm and beat a hasty retreat. Then I peered into the shower cubicle.

The creature had vanished, merging perfectly with the grey of the floor! But there was no way I was going to get back into the shower; it was either it or me. I brought out the Hit and sprayed it liberally on the floor. Ah, there it was, wriggling and writhing with its hideous hairy legs and sickle-like pincers. But it didn't seem to be in any distress, in fact, it now looked intoxicated and was thirsting for battle again.

I had no choice: I brought out the big gun: the toilet brush.

If there is one creepy crawly I have a horror of, it is this: the centipede. I have read about how painful and venomous its sting could be and man, did it have attitude! I've kept the toilet brush close at hand and have had to use it once subsequently. I even discovered that one way to winkle it out of hiding was to turn on the shower—it doesn't seem to like being sprayed. Even now I keep a wary eye out while in the shower.

Actually, as I later discovered, most of my fears were unfounded. Yes, the centipede has a very painful bite, and a terrible attitude, but its venom cannot really harm us unless we are allergic to bee stings—or if we are a small child. (A few species can be dangerous to us though as their bites can even lead to gangrene.) But yes, you'll be in trouble if you're a cockroach, locust, beetle, fly or suchlike insect pest because that's what it's really after. If you are one of these, then you better run! Or else it'll sprint after you, pounce, stab you with its massive pincers (adapted legs actually), inject you with venom, and then horror of horrors, embrace you with its bristling moustache of legs and eat you. This method of capture is called lassoing. These hairy horrors are out and out carnivores.

Just be grateful that these creatures have shrunk drastically in size since prehistoric times. While their earliest fossils date back to 430 million years ago, the largest that we know of was a monster 1 metre in length that terrorized small creatures 300 million years ago. Can you imagine one of those crawling out of the shower plughole and heading for you at high speed? Today, the largest is the giant Amazonian centipede large enough at 30 cm long and not something you'd like to tangle with either; it hunts lizards, rodents, small birds and even bats.

Centipedes were one of the earliest creatures to make the transition from water to land. And while their name might mean 'a hundred feet', no centipede species has exactly hundred feet. Their bodies are made up of numerous segments—always in odd numbers—and each segment (they have a minimum of fifteen) has a pair of legs. Their heads are rounded or flattened and armed with fearsome mandibles (the first two legs actually) and long feelers, with which they sense or sniff out their prey. Some may not have eyes, but others do, though according to some researchers they can't see very well. According to others, they see perfectly well! They've topped out at 354 legs which are good enough, and will make any footwear salesperson smile when they go shopping for shoes. Along their length, from head to tail, the legs get longer at each segment so the creatures don't trip over their own feet while rushing to attack you.

Estimates vary as to how many species there are, ranging from 8000 to 10,000 'known to science'. So far just 3000 have been 'described' by science. They emerge at night and prefer living in damp, dark locations. Their cuticle (skin) is kind of open to the air so they're very susceptible to dehydration, hence they love the damp and dank and therefore an affinity to bathrooms and basements. They're found pretty much all over the world in varying habitats from deserts to tropical rainforests.

When they want to have babies, gentlemen centipedes lay down a packet of sperm in a silken case on the ground and then entice the lady to lie on top of it and imbibe the sperm packet and its contents into her body. She may subsequently lay between ten and sixty eggs (again estimates vary) and some moms do look after their babies after they've hatched. But if matters get dire, like it becomes very dry, or a predator lurks close, she may eat them herself. On average, centipedes live five to six years, some go on to ten. Centipedes searching for partners may leave a phospherent trail in their wake as they crawl up walls or other surfaces.

Centipedes are themselves hunted by birds, rodents, meerkats, snakes, and even ants, and are eaten by us in China. Here, as well as in Laos, Thailand and Cambodia, large centipedes are immersed in liquor and drunk as an invigorating 'medicine'.

To prevent being eaten, centipedes have good getaway speed (1.3 feet per second, or 0.886 mph or 1.4 kmph), a fearsome, venomous bite, and can leave a trail of unpleasant substances in their wake to put off pursuers. These may include hydrogen cyanide, which is not something you'd like to sniff. They can also shed their legs when attacked, wriggling free of a bird and leaving it with a hairy moustache full of spiky feet—not appetizing at all.

Normally, centipedes dress in drab colours like brown, black, beige, and grey, though some are marked out in scarlet and other bright shades. They moult throughout their lives, adding segments (and legs) with each new avatar, especially after they've lost a few legs to predators.

Now that I know that what centipedes are really after, and that I am neither cockroach nor locust nor fly, what's my attitude towards them going to be? No, I am certainly not going to share the shower with them, and they'll have to go. But maybe instead of opening fire with the toilet brush I should get myself a handy, long pair of tweezers so I can pick them up and chuck them in the flower beds where I'm sure they'll be just as happy. But yes, it would help if they improved that bristling belligerent attitude.

'Millipede', as you might have guessed, means 'a thousand feet' in Latin, and are also known as 'thousand leggers'. And yes, while they certainly outnumber centipedes in this department, not a single millipede species has thousand legs. They've topped out at 750 legs (usually between 100 and 400), more than enough to make yet another footwear salesperson dance with joy.

Millipedes are also very ancient creatures, with fossils dating back between 419.2 and 443.8 million years ago, and early versions were over 2 metres long! The reduction in their size and that of other creepy crawlies is due to the reduction in oxygen levels in the atmosphere over millions of years. Millipedes are only distantly related to centipedes and very different really. Firstly, their bodies are also made up of segments, but each segment has four pairs of feathery legs attached to it, two on either side. Also, millipedes are largely vegans or more likely scavengers, eating rotting stuff, leaves, plant juices, etc in the soil. They especially like plants rich in calcium and are useful in calcium cycling. Disgustingly, but usefully, they also eat their own feces because of the useful gut bacteria it contains which helps their digestion. Millipedes are very useful in soil composting and in some situations even better than earthworms. They may bore, wedge or burrow into the soil in order to dig holes and thus play a big role in soil decomposition. Very few species of millipedes are predatory.

There are 12,000 identified species with up to an estimated 80,000 in the world. In India, we've identified just 270 species but that's because not many people are researching them. Typically, millipedes are dull coloured (some have bright shades), live on the forest floor virtually all over the world, except Antarctica, and in some forests may be crammed 1000 individuals per square metre! Some can survive underwater for eleven months.

In other ways, they are similar to centipedes: they have problems with water loss so prefer dank and damp environments and millipede dads also 'make out' indirectly with their ladies by leaving their sperm packets on the ground for the ladies to squat on. Millipede moms may lay between 100 and 300 eggs and usually desert them, though some do look after them till they hatch. Babies are born with just three pairs of legs, so have their work cut out for them while they moult and grow! The largest at present may be 20 cm long.

Millipedes fall prey to birds, small mammals, reptiles, small amphibians and have developed ways of protecting themselves. Some curl up into a tight ball and most emit foul, defensive chemicals which can be toxic and caustic. (In one species, they are toxic enough for the famous poison-dart frogs of South America to imbibe them for their own protection!) The predators often rub the millipedes hard against the ground to get rid of these substances before consuming them. In Madagascar, lemurs and capuchin monkeys deliberately rub millipedes all over their bodies: the offensive chemicals serve as an insecticide and keep the mosquitoes at bay. Lemurs also get hopelessly intoxicated by these chemicals, and sway about drunkenly in the trees before falling asleep. Needless to say, they love the stuff! The secretions of at least one species of millipedes are known to inhibit the division of cancer cells in humans.

Millipedes are slow movers in comparison to centipedes, though like them, their weird wave-like motion (all those legs moving in synchrony) can seem pretty creepy.

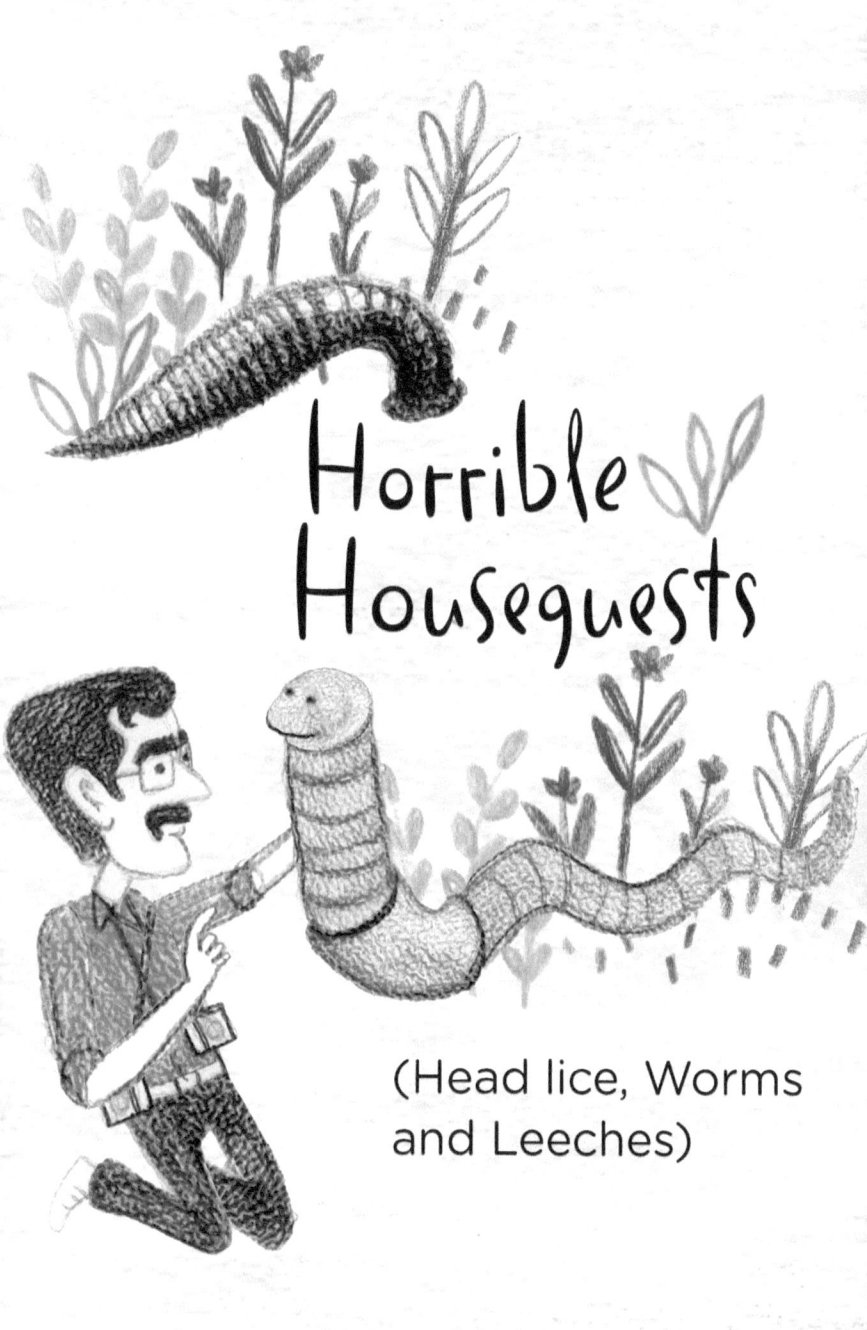

Horrible Houseguests

(Head lice, Worms and Leeches)

We, kind and generous human beings, host some truly horrible houseguests. Some just visit us in the dead of night as though we are late-opening bars: they drink to their hearts' content and disappear. (Bedbugs, for example, that we have dealt with in an earlier chapter). Others latch on to us, clinging to our hair and other parts of our bodies. And then there are those which go right where all the food action takes place inside our bodies in our intestines and establish residences there as though we were running a long-term home-stay residence for them with free board and lodging. Finally, there are those that hump out of wet places— lakes, swamps, the grassy, mossy banks around water bodies—latch on to us and drink deeply before dropping off with soft, soggy thumps, when filled up.

All are ghastly, but not all are harmful.

Head Lice

At some point or the other during your childhood, your mom would have called you to her, sat you down and gone through your hair with a fine-tooth comb. She might have done this also with grown-up relatives with long tresses. But for some reason, head lice seem to particularly love children, possibly because kids play together, sit together in school, eat together and put their heads together while solving impossible algebraic equations. These hideous little insects can jump from one host to another and infest whole groups of children.

On the plus side: head lice, also called chewing lice, don't suck your blood (or your brains) but feed off dead skin (dandruff) and detritus in hair and feathers. A particular species will stick to its particular 'host', animal, human or bird. They will make you scratch your head like crazy. There are special washes and shampoos which get rid of them though sometimes, parents simply shave their kids bald as a mushroom top to ensure none remain. Head lice have been bothering us since medieval times, and their presence is often taken as a sign of lack of hygiene.

Birds seem to get rid of lice by sand-bathing: you may have seen flocks of sparrows or doves squatting in a dry, sandy flower bed or sandpit, wriggling ecstatically and beating their wings as they try and get the pests off them. Some squat on ants' nests causing the ants to douse them with formic acid which does the job!

There are other kinds of lice which may infest us as we grow to adulthood, like body lice, which do indeed suck up blood, and which can pass on the typhus virus. Scientists and researchers are now linking the types of lice we have to confirm the evolutionary process. Both chimpanzees and gorillas have them (of different species)—and they are our nearest living relatives. Both types of lice had the same ancestor and split up some 6 to 7 million years ago which was about the same time as when chimpanzees split up from our humanoid family. Gorillas and humans have shared lice for 3 to 4 million years. Interestingly, it's from lice that we can even estimate how many years ago we first began to wear clothes! You see, body lice feed on clothing (as well as our bodies), and these guys separated from their common ancestor between 80,000 and 170,000 years ago, which is probably when we started feeling shy (and cold) and covered ourselves with animal skins and furs.

Lice moms lay their eggs—between three and four per day—in hair or feathers, firmly gluing them to the hair or feather with special secretions. These tiny white things are called nits. Head lice have a lifespan of one month.

While they're hugely irritating, head lice are not dangerous and in fact can trigger the body's immune system to attack that other more dangerous kind: body lice, which can pass on disease.

Ah, yes, the singular of lice is louse, so you now know where the lovely word 'lousy' comes from!

Worms

'Help! Snakes! Snakes! I have snakes!' The screams emanated from the bathroom from which my younger sister erupted, looking horrified. My mom probably did the closer examination and discovered that what my sister had passed out were just worms. I'm not sure which kind but probably they must have been tapeworms.

There are thousands of species of worms, in fact as many as 6000 species of tapeworms themselves, so we'll just deal with two of the biggest nuisances—the tapeworm and roundworm, as well as one 'good' useful variety: the earthworm.

Tapeworms look like small flattened grains of rice all connected together in a chain rather like the carriages of a train. Each little section, called a proglottid, basically consists of a bag of eggs with a life support system attached and can live a pretty much independent life when broken off, and finding its own way in the world. This happens when the animal or human does potty and unfortunately there are some creatures (like pigs) which may snuffle up this disgusting meal. Or they might just be left in the grass which cattle and sheep feed on. These animals become the 'intermediate' hosts of the tapeworm. From the digestive tracts of these animals the larvae drill their way out into other parts of the body like the muscle. Here they form flaccid balloon-like cysts which are filled with fluid and inside which the tapeworm develops. If we in turn eat these animals undercooked as pork, beef, lamb or fish or poultry, the larvae pass on to us and fully develop here, in their permanent home. Adult tapeworms live and breed in our intestines for long periods of time (as many as thirty years), growing to obscene lengths, as much as 25 metres long. They attach themselves to our intestines with suckers at the head and tail end and absorb nutrients with their whole bodies. When each 'egg sac' or proglottid is mature, it is shed and the whole cycle begins again.

Tapeworms in the intestine rarely cause us harm, even though the prospect of hosting them may be revolting. It's called an intestinal infection. Some people do suffer from symptoms such as weight and appetite loss, nausea, diarrhea, and dizziness. Not too long ago, sanitized tapeworms were being offered to ladies as a weight-loss treatment, one advertisement catchily reading, 'Fat, the enemy…that is banished! How? By sanitized tapeworms! Jar packed. No ill effects!'

With medication it is easy to get rid of a tapeworm infestation in the gut. In fact, as children, we were probably all 'de-wormed' as were our pets.

What is certainly dangerous is if you ingest tapeworm eggs through eating infected, undercooked food such as pork or drinking contaminated water. Because now the eggs hatch into larvae inside your gut, burrow out of it and may make their way into various organs and tissues and form cysts there, causing damage. If they reach the brain, they may cause serious neurological problems such as seizures, meningitis and worse. This is called having an 'invasive infection'.

Of course, the simplest way to avoid trouble is to cook your food, especially meat, fish and poultry, well and boil and filter your drinking water. So it's best to avoid rare, bloody steaks and pork chops, no matter how macho eating that may seem to be. Also, while trekking in the great outdoors, it's best not to casually scoop up a palm full of cool, clear mountain water from a stream and drink it straight: god knows how many animals may have pooped in the water upstream and you won't be able to see any tapeworm eggs if they are present. So do boil for at least ten minutes to get rid of them and any other nasties.

Roundworms

These comprise a vast clan of 40,000 species, though scientists are still arguing over the numbers. They're generally small and very slender, growing perhaps to 1 metre in length. (One source said they may be thick as a pencil and 1 foot long.) They are very unpleasant parasites that live in our intestines and can pass on a number of very nasty diseases depending on their species. They are armed with a sharp stylet (a very thin needle) with which they stab their prey and which may be hollow to enable them suck up nutrients. We can get infected with these lovelies through the mouth by eating or drinking infected food and water or more insidiously even through the skin by walking on infected soil or too closely hugging a pet. (Most dogs have roundworms at some time or the other). Once in the intestines they can be lodgers for two years. They have a weird kind of life cycle: if a child swallows a roundworm egg, it will hatch into a baby worm or larva in the intestine. From here it will burrow its way out and make its way via the lungs into the throat. Here it is swallowed yet again and finds itself back in the intestine where it lives as an adult for the rest of its life.

The different varieties of roundworms can give you different diseases: you may have a hookworm infection (usually got by walking barefoot on infected soil) or pinworms or something called trichinosis, which affects muscle tissues. Symptoms of a worm infestation include diarrhea, weakness, serious anemia, stomach pain and cramps and in children wheezing, coughing, loss of appetite, fever, weight loss and slow growth. Fortunately, with the correct treatment you can be rid of these nasties in just a week.

Earthworms

See, there's hope for you (and me): We can be called worms by trolls, but not all worms are nasties. Some (like us) are noble! In fact, no less than Charles Darwin had this to say about earthworms: *'it may be doubted whether there are any other animals which have played so important a part in the history of the world as have these lowly organized creatures'.*

Happily, there seem to be enough of them to go around, some 6000 species that are found around the world, and which may be crammed 1.75 million to the acre in rich soils. True to their name, they live on, in and under the soil and have neatly divided their living spaces in accordance with their diet.

Thus, with earthworms, we have those who live on and in the leaf litter where it meets the soil and do not burrow under the soil, and eat decomposing organic matter. Then there are those who live on the topsoil and eat the soil too, casting horizontal burrows in the soil at depths between 10 and 30 cm. Finally there are those that dig deep, and sink vertical burrows from which they rise to feed on the leaf litter on the surface.

Usually, earthworms are brown and wriggly, averaging 14 inches (35.5 cm) long though the longest discovered so far was a whopper 10 metres long found lurking in the Mekong River delta. It takes baby earthworms—born fully formed—about a year to reach their full size. And each earthworm can be both a mama and papa at the same time, fertilizing each other and having each other's babies (around two to twenty)! Some can reproduce even without fertilization. They breathe through their skins and are acutely sensitive to touch especially recoiling at the feel of anything salty such as a sweaty human hand. (It can fatally dehydrate them.) They can't really see but are sensitive to light and dark. In the wild, they may live up to eight years. Earthworm partners meet each other with the help of pheromones (their equivalent of 'come hither' perfumes). Their babies are stronger than the adults as they are able to push 500 times their weight, their parents managing to push just 10 times theirs'. If they lose a segment they can regenerate it—which would be so wonderful if we could do likewise to a lost or amputated limb!

Farmers and gardeners have long cherished earthworms because of the way they deal with the soil. With their burrows, they aerate the soil allowing the passage of air in and out as well as providing drainage channels for water. They chew up and digest particles of sand and grit in their gizzard and then digest them. They have enormous appetites eating (and excreting) their own weight in food and waste every day! Their excreted 'casts' deposited on the surface or under the soil are five times richer in nitrogen, seven times richer in phosphates and eleven times richer in potassium than is found in the top 6 inches of normal soil: so talk about it being a health food for plants! Decomposing leaf litter is likewise partially digested and turned into nourishment for the soil. The fertility of the soil increases and more plants can grow. You can often see earthworm casts on the surface of your lawn or in flower beds especially during the rains. In ideal living conditions, each earthworm is capable of producing 4.5 kg of casts every year! In fact, 'vermiculture'—the use of earthworms to convert organic waste into fertilizer—has become a big business these days. They have also been used to revitalize degraded soils of which there seems to be a lot of in India.

Sadly, earthworms have legions of enemies: birds that slurp them up like noodles, and animals which may include bears, foxes, hedgehogs, wild pigs as well as invertebrates like ants, beetles, slugs, snails and spiders. We feed them to fish, poultry and pigs because they're rich in protein. They fall foul of parasites too and cannot tolerate nitrogenous fertilizers, forget about pesticides such as DDT.

But perhaps the worst indignity we subject them to, is when we dig them out of the ground and impale them, wriggling and squirming, on viciously barbed fishhooks and then throw them into the water at the end of the line. Really, some respect would be in order here!

Leeches

If you've ever been on a hike or trek to a wild place or forest, especially near water like a stream or river or lake or marsh, you are likely to have encountered these lovelies, more so if you've actually waded through the shallows. Sometimes alas, you'll find them lurking in very private nooks and crannies of your body and which will make you scream. They're black or dark reddish-brown glutinious looking worm-like creatures which have their heads or tails (they have suckers at both ends) buried in your body and as you keep looking (if you can) will visibly bloat as they swell up with your blood. Worry not, for they'll be all tanked up in between twenty minutes to an hour and then just drop off with a soggy thud though you will continue to bleed for a while till the effect of the anticoagulant wears off. They don't pass on any germs to us usually, but could cause allergic reactions and anemia if you are attacked by a whole battalion of them.

Leeches have a horrible way of humping across terrain and on to you, which is called 'looping'. Or else they will swiftly swim across a pond or stream towards you. They can either stab you with their proboscis, or saw into you with a triple-bladed jaw depending on their species, making a Y-shaped incision in your skin. They will first anesthetize the site (though there is still some doubt about whether they actually do) and inject an anticoagulant, so the blood flows freely and you feel nothing. There are nearly 700 species found all over the world, excepting Antarctica, the largest being a nightmarish 30 cm long and most don't really care about whose blood they suck! They are related to their noble cousins the earthworms, and like them each leech is both a mama and papa at the same time.

The most famous and best-known species of leeches is the medicinal leech, and like its name implies, it has been used by surgeons and doctors for 2500 years till around the middle of the nineteenth century for blood-letting. They have been mentioned by the Greeks and Ayurvedic physicians. Recently, surgeons have been using them in micro-surgery, where they have to work with delicate blood vessels that tend to get turgid with blood and so difficult to operate on. If god forbid, you need a cut-off finger or toe re-attached, leeches can be used to reduce the swelling of the tissues at the site and restore blood circulation after the surgeons re-attach the limb. A substance found in the saliva of leeches is also being used to dissolve blood clots. Medicinal leeches need just two blood meals a year to keep them happy.

If you find leeches on your body after a trek, don't try to yank them off, as they might just break off leaving their heads buried inside you. Salt will make them let go as they get dehydrated, and so does cigarette smoke though that'll mean opening a whole new can of worms! Perhaps the best thing you could do while on a trek is to wear long socks, long trousers and keep your sleeves rolled down.

Appalling Animal Lovers

(Ticks and Fleas)

Anyone who has kept dogs or cats as pets would have encountered them: hideous, reddish-brown tiny disc-shaped creatures, latched on tightly to your pet's fur (if they've drunk their fill of blood they'll be like soft grey-green barrage balloons) and tiny reddish-brown oval insects scuttling for cover before you can do anything about them. Most pets have them: ticks and fleas.

We'll deal with ticks first. There are actually two great clans—hard-bodied ticks (which your pets get) of which there are about 700 species, and soft-bodied ticks (who like cattle and livestock and birds) of which there are around 200 species. Both live on blood meals and both can spread unpleasant diseases. Occasionally, both will also check us out.

Years ago, in Mumbai, when we got our first dog, a boxer we called Bambi, our mom used to remind me and my sisters everyday, to 'please check Bambi for ticks'. Which we dutifully did because Mumbai, being warm and humid, was a haven for ticks. Sure enough we would, with the help of tweezers, remove about ten or twelve of the horrors from her fur and had to be especially careful of checking her neck, ears and the soft areas between the pads of her paws. She was a sweet, obedient dog who would come and sit down in front of us with a sigh as we ran our fingers through her fur, parting it to make sure there were none. If the ticks had fed, they gained in size and weight by 200 to 600 times, and you could feel them as hideous soft lumps on her fur. After yanking them out, we would with great relish drop them in a can of kerosene (called 'Bambi's pickle-jar') and watch with satisfaction as they sank to the bottom.

Well, one summer we must have been a bit lax because one morning we discovered that instead of the usual score, she had over fifty of the little horrors. And when we looked inside her ear flaps, we were horrified: they were beaded with them, all fat as balloons, and some had gone fairly deep inside. We had noticed that Bambi had become a little listless and lethargic and not as sprightly as she normally was. We rang the vet. He prescribed some foul-smelling liquid pesticide, which we were to dilute and bathe her with and told us to check the house. Sure enough, we discovered ticks on the curtains, in cracks in the walls and then hit the motherlode: Bambi's sofa, where she slept. It was crawling with them, they were using this as a sort of dharamshala. All soft furnishings had to be thrown out and the entire flat fumigated. But happily, Bambi was soon her usual bouncy self. She could have contracted tick fever and even died had we been more amiss. Of course, we were very careful and thorough after that.

Ticks are in fact related to spiders and scorpions and have eight legs. They are extremely hardy and resilient creatures and can withstand extremes of temperature: they can tolerate -18 degrees Celsius for up to two hours and temperatures between -7 and -2 degrees Celsius for up to two weeks. Also, they can live in drought conditions for as long as eighteen months. Ideally, however, they prefer warm, humid climates, though they can be found all around the world, including Antarctica where they feed on the blood of penguins. By hitching lifts on migratory birds they spread all over: if you've ever caught a bird in a net (for any purpose) it's best to check it for ticks and other parasites. Ticks developed an appetite for blood some 120 million years ago and need a blood meal to go through the various stages of their lives. They may take between ten minutes and two hours over their meals.

They will pierce their host's skin with a harpoon-like needle (made of calcium carbonate), inject an anticoagulant and anesthetic and suck up the blood. They can remain undetected on their host for eight to ten days—or until the time you check the host! They find their victims through odour, body heat, the animal's exhalations and vibrations. One method of latching on is rather sinisterly called, 'questing'. The tick clings on to vegetation say a leaf or twig or grass stem and waves its forelegs around, sensing the presence of the animal. When it comes close enough, or brushes against the foliage, the tick detaches from its perch and clings on to its host, burying itself in its fur. That's why it's important to check your dog thoroughly after it's had a run in a grassy field or meadow. Hard-bodied ticks stick tightly to their hosts until they've gorged themselves to up to 600 times their original size and then drop off. Soft-bodied ticks, which do not stick, drop off after they're ten times their original size, and await their next victim. Ticks have been divided into whether they're 'one-host', 'two-host' or 'three-host'. Adult female, 'one-host' ticks will feed until they're ready to lay eggs and then drop off.

Newly hatched larvae latch on to a host for a blood meal and in turn develop into 'nymphs' which continue the feeding orgy and which in turn change into adults.

The larvae of 'two-host' ticks also seek out a blood meal, develop into nymphs and continue to feed. But once engorged, they drop off and wait to moult into their adult form before finding a second host.

The eggs of 'three-host' ticks (most hard-bodied ticks) are laid by the thousands on the ground by their mom, where they hatch into larvae, which seek out small animals and birds and latch on to these. Here, they feed and fatten and then detach themselves in order to moult into pupae on the ground. Now they seek out a second host on which to feed and after they do, gorge themselves yet again and fall off onto the ground. They moult into adults, which in turn seek out a third host to feed on, and a mate. Once mated, the female drops off to the ground to lay her eggs and so the circle of life goes on.

Scientists are studying tick saliva (they would, wouldn't they!) which contains between 1500 and 3000 proteins and have anti-inflammatory properties, which could prove useful to us in treatment of heart disease, by preventing inflammation of the heart muscle. (This is what enables ticks to remain undetected on their hosts.)

Ticks can pass on several very unpleasant diseases including typhus, the dreaded Kyasanur Forest Disease (also called monkey fever) which occurs only in south-west India and can be very serious, as well as various types of tick fever both in humans and animals. But ticks do need long feeding sessions in order to pass on the pathogens. While some birds do peck them off grazing animals, guinea-fowl and opossums find them extremely appetizing.

While hiking through a forest, it's best to wear long-sleeved shirts and to tuck your trousers into your socks, and if you've taken your dog along, to check it thoroughly. Tick (and flea) powders and collars are also readily available, which might help, though there's nothing like a thorough hand-check.

Fleas are the other big nuisances that plague our pets—both animals and birds. They're small, oval, brown creatures, that scuttle about lithely in the depths of the fur and which are almost impossible to catch with your fingers. If you do manage to catch one, you'll soon realize how difficult it is to squeeze it to death as it's hard and resistant and the moment you release pressure will leap away and vanish! It can also cling on forcefully, with the help of its claws, so dislodging it is not easy.

There are about 2500 to 3000 species of fleas in the world and like ticks, they live on blood. They can't fly but they can leap up to fifty times their own body length, with the help of very powerful hind legs. They developed between 145 and 66 million years ago and each flea species has its own preferred host on which it feeds and breeds.

They have hard, flattened bodies, covered with hairs and little spikes pointing backwards which assist them to scuttle around in their hosts' fur or feathers. Their tough exoskeleton helps them to be impervious to the furious scratching of their hosts. But the flea's most unique physical property is its ability to jump. Its leg muscles, by themselves, are not strong enough to provide the energy required for the leap, so fleas adopt much the same method as grasshoppers and locusts do to jump. They slowly contract their powerful leg muscles, storing the energy in an elastic pad of protein called reslin, rather like you do when you pull back a bow string and bend the bow. There's a catch which prevents the premature release of the energy, but when the flea lets go, like you let go of the arrow, it flies a distance of 18 cm and so rapidly you don't see it!

Lady fleas can lay up to 5000 eggs in a lifetime, which go through the typical four-stage process of egg, larva, pupa and adult. Gruesomely, it has been found that 90 per cent of the larvae hatch into adults—if they have fed on unviable eggs, which I guess is a form of cannibalism! With a healthy diet of blood, fleas can live for up to one and half years, though typically their lifespan is only between one and two months. They like it to be warm and humid. Fleas like to breed near the sleeping quarters of their hosts, so it's sensible to wash your dog's bed regularly. One theory about why humans don't have much (or any) body hair was that this evolved in order to free us from pestiferous ticks and fleas.

While flea bites can cause allergies and itching, they can also pass on a host of very unpleasant and dangerous diseases. The most notorious of these is of the bubonic plague and Plague of Justinian by infected rat flea, which killed off nearly a third of Europe's population in the middle ages. Over 200 million people died between 1346 and 1671, and the great plague of London accounted for 100,000 in a single year: 1665. Of course, we thought it was a good idea to use the virus as a weapon of war, which the Japanese did in World War II to the Chinese. Plague caused a scare in India, in Surat, some years back. Luckily, only about a dozen or so species may attack us. Among the most common is the cat flea, which burrows in the soft areas between our toes and the cracks in our feet. If neglected, infestations in their hundreds may occur and it is not a pleasant prospect.

Heavy-duty vacuuming of the areas fleas are likely to be found in like carpets, rugs, and the beds of pets can reduce their occurrence as well as scrupulous hygiene and the dusting of flea powders on your pet.

In the old days, the concept of the flea circus became a popular form of entertainment and in fact is still around today in the west! Fleas were hitched on to and made to pull miniature carriages and carts with the help of fine gold threads and given uniforms to wear. They 'performed' in tiny circus sets, their natural proclivity to jump probably adding to the entertainment value. This pastime was especially popular with jewelers and watchmakers who wanted to show off their ability to miniaturize everything!

Afterword

Now you know that there's a vast array of wonderful, kaleidoscopic creatures out there for you to meet and get to know about. Their role in our lives is vital for our survival, so treat them with respect even if they insist on biting and stinging you! Each one of them is perfectly and precisely designed and equipped for the role they must play in the world and to pass on their genes to the next generation. Many have qualities that Superman would envy. Sure, many are dangerous to our health and have caused havoc in society so they need to be dealt with carefully. The ones described in this book are just a sampling of some of the more commonly met. There are some 400,000 species of just beetles out there: go on and make at least one of them your own! Remember, you can have a 'lifer' every day—or maybe even every hour! Beat that!

TERMITES digest wood—we can't.
- Termites invented central air conditioning.
- Termites: 2; Humans: 0

ANTS may have armies and go to war. Some even 'treat' their injured on the battlefield.
- Ants have strict passport and visa controls at the entrance to their colonies. No immigrants!
- The jaws of some soldier ants have been used by surgeons to 'staple' open wounds. Of course, they cut off the ants' heads first. Charming, aren't we?

COCKROACHES may be the only survivors of a nuclear holocaust. Serves us right!

There are more species of **BEETLES** than any other living species.
- Dung-beetles may use the light from the Milky Way to navigate their way.
- Australia would have been neck deep in dung if it had not been for (imported) dung-beetles.
- Some beetles can get through sheets of copper and zinc.
- Bombardier beetles have machine-gun bottoms.

WHIRLIGIGS use radar to target their prey.

Great clusters of **LADYBIRDS** can be found under snow-drifts. Cool, eh?

LADY PRAYING MANTIS, headlong in love, enjoys a delicious honeymoon: Lord Mantis, head-first!
- Baby mantids have a tough childhood: they may be eaten by mamma or their siblings.

DRAGONFLIES may have 30,000 lenses in each compound eye. What great fun when they have to put on their contact lenses!
- They can fly and strike their targets mid-air at 90 kmph.

Gluttony, abstinence, meditation, shape-shifting: **BUTTERFLIES** and **MOTHS** have been there and done it all. And most enjoy blood, sweat, tears, dung, festering flesh, rum, and nectar, of course.
- The monarch butterfly migrates 4500 km from North America and Canada to a small patch of forest in Mexico in the winter. On the way back it takes three generations of monarchs to reach back home. How do the newbies know what they have to do and in which direction they must fly? Hmm...

- Scientists are still figuring out exactly why moths dive-bomb naked bulbs in kamikaze flights.

HONEYBEES may dance, quack, toot, and are possibly sentient. They pollinate one-third of our food.

Some **WASPS** anaesthetize their prey so that their larvae have a supply of fresh live meat 24X7.
- The larval grubs will eat their meal carefully: vital organs are left for last so the meal remains alive for the longest!
- The miniscule fig wasp pollinates the giant banyan tree—clearly size doesn't matter.

A swarm of **LOCUSTS** can wipe out a small country's entire grain stock in a single strike

SPIDER silk may be able to stop a 747 in mid-flight!
- Spiderlings leave home by parasailing.

MOSQUITOES have killed more of us than all of our own best efforts to kill each other.

FLIES wash their 'hands' before eating but then vomit all over their meal (to turn it into a smoothie) before consuming it. Try doing this at a Michelin-starred restaurant!

MAGGOTS have saved wounded soldiers on the battlefield by cleaning up the dead tissue around their wounds, preventing gangrene and consequent loss of limbs. They don't dig live tissue.

RAT FLEAS spread the bubonic plague that wiped out nearly one-third of the population in Europe.

Smooch! The **KISSING BUG** will smooch you on your eyelids and near your lips while you are fast asleep at night.

No **CENTIPEDE** has exactly 100 legs; no millipede exactly 1000.

Surgeons use **LEECHES** in micro-surgery.

Charles Darwin maintained that perhaps no other creature has played as important part a role in the history of the world as the lowly **EARTHWORM**.

Insects contain more protein weight for weight than beef, mutton, pork, fish, and of course dal-sabzi and millets. So do order stir fry cockroaches, roasted dragonflies and crispy grasshoppers along with stewed bluebottles the next time you eat out. It's good for you!

www.ingramcontent.com/pod-product-compliance
Lightning Source LLC
LaVergne TN
LVHW041702070526
838199LV00045B/1170